Patchwork & Appliqué

ENIGMA BOOKS

Previous page: A detail from a nineteenth century bedspread known as the Baltimore Bride's quilt. Many of the American quilts of this era were made by a combination of patchwork and appliqué.

Right: Modern patchwork cushions, in which a variety of printed fabrics have been combined to form Log Cabin and large-scale triangle designs.

Overleaf: A child's appliqué quilt with bold, colourful motifs. The shapes were sewn to the background squares with machine zigzag stitch.

US terminology is indicated in the text by [ ] brackets.

Edited by Sarah Parr

Text compiled by Pamela Tubby

**Published by Marshall Cavendish
Books Limited**
58 Old Compton Street
London W1V 5PA

© Marshall Cavendish Limited 1970
-71-72-73-74-75-76-77

First printed 1977

Printed in Great Britain

Some of this material has previously
appeared in other Marshall
Cavendish publications

ISBN 0 85685 253 8

Introduction

Patchwork and appliqué are sister crafts that have been enjoyed by needlewomen for centuries. Generations of enthusiastic beginners have been drawn to them by the desire to create unique items and preserve precious scraps of fabric.

Today, new machine techniques and an ever-increasing range of textiles have brought new dimensions to these absorbing needle arts. The inspiring color photographs in this book illustrate the wide variety of stunning items that can be made with patchwork and appliqué – tablecloths, clothes, cushions and crib blankets, as well as traditional quilts, are just some of them.

Patchwork and Appliqué guides the beginner through all the important preliminaries of these two crafts – collecting tools and equipment, choosing suitable fabrics, and planning designs. Once the basic patchwork techniques have been mastered, dozens of beautiful patterns can be created from the geometric shapes. You will also enjoy experimenting with the traditional designs that have their own special techniques – Log Cabin, Mayflower, Crazy Work and Suffolk Puffs.

Appliqué is a needle art of exciting possibilities. It can be as practical or as decorative as you wish – from a simple motif on a quilt cover to a lavish wall hanging decorated with embroidery. So whether you are adding a motif to a pair of jeans, learning about San Blas reverse appliqué or co-ordinating furnishings with appliqué Perse – you will soon discover its versatility.

Patchwork and appliqué are absorbing, creative and satisfying crafts. Once you have browsed through this book you will long to start sewing. Make your leisure hours relaxing and rewarding by creating highly individual items which will be a pleasure to use and a joy to treasure.

Contents

Chapter 1
Introduction to patchwork

The history of patchwork

Like many crafts, patchwork was born of necessity and through the ages developed into an intricate and complex folk art. No one knows its true origins, but it must have developed soon after weaving, when every scrap of cloth was precious and even the tiniest pieces could be re-joined to create a new fabric. Shaping and re-arranging these scraps to make patterns was the next logical step in its 'evolution'.

Early history

Patchwork is believed to have been introduced into Europe by the Crusaders. In time it spread to all the countries around the Mediterranean and across the continent. Pictures in medieval manuscripts show banners and tunics decorated in a way which indicates a knowledge of patchwork and appliqué. In England, patchwork developed alongside embroidery, appliqué and quilting, all of which are part of a long unbroken tradition of skilful needlework.

Through the centuries patchwork was a part of every day domestic economy. The earliest surviving English examples only date back about 250 years, as many earlier pieces must have worn out through constant daily use.

One of the earliest surviving pieces of patchwork in the world is an Egyptian funeral pall made from pieces of gazelle hide, pre-dating the modern fashion for leather patchwork by about 3000 years.

Even more fascinating is a discovery made during an archeological expedition exploring the remote regions beyond the River Ganges in the 1920s. A walled-up chapel was found in The Caves of the Thousand Buddhas, situated on the old trade route linking the silk growing provinces of China with central Asia and the west.

Inside the chapel were many pieces of patchwork including a large votive hanging made from many-coloured rectangles of silk. It was probably stitched together by a priest from offerings of silk left at the shrine by travellers.

All the patchwork found in the chapel was made by oversewing the patches together on the wrong side in exactly the same way we do today, linking its craftsmen with modern patchwork enthusiasts in an unbroken tradition over thousands of years.

Types of patchwork

True pieced, or mosaic patchwork is made from fragments of cloth which are stitched together to create a whole new fabric. All-over mosaic designs have generally been more popular in England, while 'block' designs are a characteristic of American patchwork. A block is one complete pattern, and a number of blocks are stitched together to create the finished article.

Patchwork has always been closely linked with appliqué, where cloth is shaped and stitched down to a background fabric. Many patterns combine mosaic patchwork with appliqué.

A number of patchwork patterns are constructed by the 'pressed' method, a mixture of patchwork and appliqué where the patches are stitched to a foundation fabric, completely covering it. Log Cabin, Pineapple and Grandmother's Fan are all made by the pressed method.

Patchwork and quilting

To many people, patchwork and quilting are synonymous. Both are equally ancient techniques and decorative quilting on plain lengths of fabric is a demanding and intricate craft with a long history. Quilting, stitching two or more layers of cloth together to make a warm covering, probably became linked with patchwork for the old reason of domestic economy. When a new length of cloth was available, it was more important to make new clothes – the old clothes could be cut up and re-joined, then quilted to a warm interlining.

In America, patchwork is most often associated with quilts. In England patchwork was also used to make other things, possibly because making a quilt also involved making the other furnishings that went with a four poster bed, for example the curtains and valances. The Victorians, in particular, used patchwork to make all sorts of furnishings, chair seat covers, tablecloths and antimacassars.

Facing previous page: Patchwork constructed by the American block method. Named after a wild plant, the Shoo-fly design is made up from nine-patch blocks, which are pieced from a combination of squares and half-square triangles.

Opposite: A detail from an eighteenth century English quilt. It illustrates the successful combination of embroidery and patchwork in rich fabrics. The total effect resembles Crazy patchwork in the random use of colour and pattern.

American patchwork

Because patchwork was such a part of everyday domestic 'make do and mend', very little is known about its development in Europe before the eighteenth century when it was elevated to a decorative needlework art and became a fashionable occupation among the more leisured middle classes. At the same time, settlers were moving out to the New World and the great tradition of American patchwork was beginning. It is said, with a great deal of truth, that the history of America is written in its patchwork quilts.

Thrifty Dutch and English housewives are credited with bringing patchwork to America. There is even a particular type of patchwork said to have been devised from the old flour sacks on the Mayflower, the ship that took the Pilgrims from England across the Atlantic.

Once in America, the settlers had to utilize every scrap of cloth they had brought with them. It would be quite a long time before any new lengths of homespun could be woven, and when they were, the cloth was needed for clothes. This situation repeated itself continually as people moved farther west.

The settlers had brought with them the patterns they had learnt at home from their mothers. As patchwork developed in the new country, patterns were adapted and new ones devised. Many women kept a record of the new patterns they saw by making up a single block and keeping it in a drawer until they were ready to make the next quilt. These collections were considered very valuable. They were intended to be passed down through the family and were often mentioned in wills.

The names given to each pattern are a characteristic of American patchwork, reflecting the political and social changes that took place. Over the years many patterns acquired a number of different names. One pattern that took its name from the small bean of a plant known as Job's Tears, became known later as Slaves' Chain. During the annexation of Texas it became Texas Tears. Other patterns reflect the movement of the settlers westward; for example Wagon Tracks, the Rocky Road to Kansas and the Road to California. New plants and animals that were encountered and the changing landscape are also reflected in patchwork. The Carolina Lily, Cactus Flower, Prairie Flower and Texas Rose are just some of the names given to different patterns.

Patchwork wove itself into the fabric of American social life. It became part of the frontier tradition of 'lending a helping hand'. Quilting Bees to complete family quilts were a neighbourly effort, like barn and house raisings and corn shuckings. The patchwork top was generally made during the winter when there were long hours free for sewing. To complete a quilt, the backing, warm interlining and patchwork top had to be quilted together while they were stretched tightly in a frame. Few houses had a warm room large enough for the eight foot frame, so the quilting was generally saved until summer when the frame could be set up outside.

It could take one person anything from two weeks to two months to quilt a top, but with help from her neighbours a woman could get a top

quilted in one day. All day the women stitched and talked and in the evening the men drove over to admire the work and round off the day with a party.

For a number of women to make a quilt was a way of expressing friendship and concern for friends and neighbours. To celebrate an engagement; honour a teacher, minister or hero; to help a family get back on its feet after a fire, or as a remembrance for settlers going west – all were occasions for quilt making and giving. Each woman would work a block of the quilt and then they would meet to stitch the blocks together and quilt the top. The presentation of the quilt was always accompanied by a party.

Masterpiece quilts

Years ago, every family whether English or American had to have their stock of quilts. There were the everyday quilts for family use and the best quilts, kept wrapped up in a sheet or spread splendidly on the bed in the guest room – only to be used by an honoured guest or on special occasions.

In America these quilts were known as Masterpiece quilts. They were made only when there were enough quilts for family use and when the worker was feeling rested and refreshed. The most skillful stitchery and the most intricate and difficult patterns went into these quilts. The Star of Bethlehem was a favourite pattern for Masterpiece quilts in many parts of America. It is a large eight point star made entirely of diamonds, the most difficult shape to fold and stitch neatly.

Marriage quilts

Every girl learnt her patchwork from her mother. In America it became the custom for an unmarried girl to make a 'baker's dozen' of patchwork or appliqué quilts ready for the time when she married. The first quilt was started when the girl was very young; it was the simplest of all and the one at which she learnt her craft. As the girl grew older, each quilt became more complex. Each one was different from the others, although all would be made along the designs handed down in her family.

When a girl became engaged to marry, she began work on the thirteenth quilt, her Marriage quilt. It would be the most intricate and beautiful of all. This quilt was the only one allowed to contain symbols of love like appliqué hearts or the interlocking circles of the pattern called Wedding Ring. Border patterns on this quilt would be plotted with special care so there would be no broken ends or twisted lines of stitching. It was an old superstition brought from England which warned that a broken border in a Marriage quilt was a certain omen of trouble.

In some areas the supersitition grew up that it was unlucky for a girl to work on her own Marriage quilt, so her friends would each make a block and bring them over to the bride's house to stitch and quilt the top. Sometimes, the friends merely presented the girl with the blocks and she and her mother finished the quilt.

English patchwork

In England too, patchwork was often a joint effort. Jane Austen worked on a quilt with her mother and sisters, and in the country during the long winter evenings the whole family, often including father and sons, would help.

In country areas a quilting frame would often be set up in a village or church hall, so that local women could drop in whenever they had time to add a few more stitches to the quilt.

As in America, patchwork reflects particular aspects of the country's history. In England, changes in the trade and manufacture of materials are revealed in surviving examples of the patchwork of the seventeenth, eighteenth and nineteenth centuries.

In the seventeenth century the introduction of brightly-coloured calicoes brought changes to the English textile trade. The anger of weavers resulted in embargoes on the importation of calico and a rise in its price. The high price did not detract from its popularity but pieces of the cottons become more precious as a result. Furnishings, in particular, became prohibitively expensive to make, so patchwork furnishings made with scraps of calico became a practical and attractive alternative.

During the eighteenth and nineteenth centuries the increasing variety of available materials, in different colours and prints, meant that patterns and styles enjoyed periods of popularity until new ones caught the imaginations of patchwork enthusiasts. Floral designs on dark backgrounds, for example, were in fashion at the end of the eighteenth century.

By the beginning of the nineteenth century, when cottons were cheap, patchwork was extremely popular.

Left: A detail from a Saw Tooth Star quilt, which was made in America in the nineteenth century.

Cotton manufacturers began to print special panels and borders to be used in Framed quilts which were made to commemorate great occasions – the Golden Jubilee of George III in 1840 and the wedding of Princess Charlotte in 1816 were two such occasions.

By the middle of the nineteenth century materials of all kinds were used for patchwork, although some of the combinations used by the Victorians were ill-chosen and did not stand up to heavy wear. Velvet was very popular for furnishings, such as cushion covers, and for Crazy Work, and ribbons were used for Log Cabin quilts.

Patchwork today

Quilting picnics are still a great feature of state fairs in rural America, while in England patchwork and quilting have continued to flourish, particularly in the country.

As there is no longer a pressing need for home-made quilts, modern innovative patchworkers have begun to explore and develop patchwork. There are literally hundreds of traditional patterns, each with its own name and history. Many people have re-discovered the pleasure of piecing them together and using their patchwork in new and different ways; for clothes, furnishings, pictures, wall hangings and soft art, as well as quilts.

The sewing machine, which caused a decline in crafts and handiwork when it first became widely available, now provides us with many short cuts. These take much of the tedium out of sewing, leaving the pleasure of designing and creating unchanged.

Patchwork today is no longer restricted to the traditional geometric shapes. Its newfound vitality is reflected in free shapes, bold colour schemes and imaginative designs.

Designing patchwork

Take time over planning your patchwork design as it can be the most absorbing and enjoyable part of this craft. Designing need not be done all at once, but can be done at various stages during the work. Before you start to cut out the patches you should have a basic idea of the finished design and the size of the completed piece of patchwork, so that you can collect all the necessary materials together. Bear in mind that a small piece of patchwork will be more effective if it is made with small patches.

If you are going to make a design using patchwork blocks, decide on the size of each block and how many you will need to complete the item. Are the blocks going to be joined together or will they be separated by strips of plain fabric? Make sure that the width of the strips balances the size of the blocks; not too wide so that the patchwork looks lost, and not too narrow so that it looks cramped. Graph paper and coloured felt tip pens are useful for roughing out the balance of a complete design and the main areas of each colour.

One way of designing, which is particularly useful if you are making a mosaic design in a variety of colours, is to use the patches (that have been cut out and basted to the papers) like pieces in a jigsaw. Move them around until you are satisfied with the arrangement. A cork or chipboard mat or card table is useful for this purpose, because you can pin the patches in position when you are satisfied with the placing of each one. You can leave them there until you are ready to sew them together. Provided you keep in mind a rough idea of your basic design, you can then do a little sewing, some designing or more sewing as the mood takes you.

Colour

Most people have an innate sense of colour which they use every day without being aware of it – for instance when they are deciding which piece of clothing to wear with another.

You may already see the colour scheme of your patchwork in your mind's eye, but you will probably find that your scrap collection will have to be sorted before you begin designing.

It may be helpful to you to know something about the principles of colour relationships which play such an important part in patchwork design.

Red, yellow and blue are the primary colours. All other colours are made from combinations of these three.

Secondary colours are made by mixing primary colours. For example, if blue and yellow are mixed in equal parts they make green: red and yellow make orange and red and blue make violet. Variations are achieved according to the balance of the primary colours. The tone of a colour is its lightness or darkness.

Colour relationships

Closely related colours make an effective design. By using, say, blue and green only, you include all the tones of blue – from very light blue to navy – and all the tones of green. You could then add the shades of aqua and turquoise which are made by mixing blue and green together.

You could try picking out two complementary colours and basing your design around them. Each colour in the spectrum has its own complementary colour, the one opposite it in the spectrum. Thus green and red, yellow and violet, blue and orange are complementary. Try putting two complementary colours of the same depth and intensity together and see how they almost vibrate.

Pick out fabrics in tones of one colour and try adding an accent of colour. Accent colours are usually bright and intense and are used in small amounts to give a flash of brilliance; for example, a bright pink among a range of dark greens and khakis, or a touch of yellow among blues and violets.

If you want to use contrasting colours, a good general rule is to keep to one dominant colour, one less dominant colour and one or two accent colours. For example, if pink is your main colour and you choose tan as the second colour, then small amounts of yellow and charcoal used as accent colours will balance and

Opposite: Take plenty of time to design your patchwork. Small items, such as these potholders, are an ideal way to experiment with techniques, patterns and colours, before attempting larger and more complex projects.

Below: The primary colours and their opposite complementary colours. Be aware of the relationships of colour when you plan your patchwork.

co-ordinate the design.

These basic principles of colour relationships will help you to understand what happens as you move the scraps of cloth around.

Perspective

Colour can be used to heighten the effect of an optical illusion. Stripes can be arranged to run along the lines of perspective in certain designs. Dark tones will make a patch appear to recede and a bright tone will bring it forward. In the Baby's Blocks pattern, for example, different colours and patterns are used to lighten and shade the combined shapes – highlighting the tops of the 'boxes' and shading the 'sides'.

A pattern of four triangles, meeting in the middle to form a square, can be highlighted more strongly on one side than the other to make the surface appear as if it is coming towards you.

Other considerations

You may find that you are limited in some way when you are choosing the colours that you would like in your patchwork. If the patchwork is to be made up into a cushion cover, quilt or any other furnishing, you must consider it in relation to all the other colours in the room. If the room is full of different colours, then pick out the most striking ones, or one or two of the main colours and use shades of these in your patchwork. If you only have one main colour in your room then you could use a striking colour in your patchwork to make a striking focal point.

Texture

A mixture of textures in patchwork can be very effective. Although you should not mix fabrics of different weights in any patchwork that is to receive hard wear, it is possible to mix weights and textures in patchwork that is intended to be more decorative. Mixing silk, velvet, corduroy, satin, knubbly tweed and corded silk in approximately the same colours can make a most exciting design.

The texture of a material often alters its colour. A patch in red velvet will look glowing and jewel-like, whereas a patch of exactly the same colour in a shiny material will seem much lighter and brighter.

Textural patchwork is most successful if you limit the number of colours and let the structure of the materials create the interest.

Left: Closely-related shades of red and mauve have been used imaginatively in the patchwork tablecloth. The large scale triangles, in a variety of prints, are set off by the plain black border.

Basic tools & suitable fabrics

Basic tools

Before you begin working on your patchwork it is a good idea to collect together all the tools you will need at some stage during the work. You probably keep most of these in your needlework basket, but templates will have to be bought or made to the size you require.

Templates

Templates are patterns used to make the shapes for the papers and patches. Traditionally a patchworker would cut them herself from cardboard, or the men of the house would cut them from metal or wood. Experienced workers prided themselves on being able to cut out accurate shapes by folding and cutting the fabric along the thread.

You can cut out squares and rectangles quite easily by following the weave, but for any other shape an accurate template is essential.

Home-made templates can be made from strong cardboard, but they will not last long, as constant cutting around them wears away the edges making them inaccurate.

Making your own templates is only worthwhile if you want to make up a small piece of patchwork, experiment with new shapes, or if you cannot buy the shape you want. Certain shapes, such as rhomboids, are not manufactured commercially.

To make accurate templates you will need: strong cardboard, a craft knife, metal rule, compasses and a protractor for measuring the angles. The next chapter of this book deals with the different patchwork shapes and explains how to draw each shape to the size you require. Draw the shape clearly and accurately onto cardboard using the rule, compasses and protractor and then cut out the shape with a craft knife. If you have the right cutting tools, permanent templates can be made from wood, plastic or sheet metal.

Buying templates Most good craft and needlework shops sell metal templates in a variety of shapes and sizes. They are usually sold in packages of two. The solid metal template, the exact size of the finished patch, is used for cutting the papers. The other in the pack is the larger window template which is used for cutting the patches. It has a clear plastic centre panel, the exact size of the patch, and a solid surround, 9mm or 6mm ($\frac{3}{8}$in or $\frac{1}{4}$in) wide, the width of the patch turning.

The window template is extremely useful, especially for use with patterned or striped fabrics, because when cutting the patches you can see exactly what the finished patch will look like, and choose which part of the pattern you want to appear on the patch. With its seam allowance, the window template also makes it easier to calculate how much fabric you will need.

Remember when you are deciding on the size of patches and buying templates that the size of any shape is measured along the length of one of its sides. For example a 5cm (2in) hexagon is 5cm (2in) long on each of its six sides, it is not 5cm (2in) wide. Similarly a 5cm (2in) diamond has four sides of that length.

Papers

Accurately cut papers ensure that the patches are exact and are held firm while sewing. Good quality writing paper or the paper from glossy magazines is the ideal weight for cotton or silk patches. Thicker fabrics may need slightly heavier papers. The paper should be firm enough for its edges to be felt within the folds of fabric when the edges are turned, but it should not be too thick or stiff or it will make the work heavy and difficult to handle.

Non-woven interfacing can be used instead of paper and left in the finished work to add firmness. If the patchwork is intended for fashion appliqué, you should always use non-woven interfacing.

Other tools

Scissors You will need two pairs of scissors for patchwork. One pair should be very sharp for cutting out the patches. Use the second pair only to cut out the papers as paper quickly blunts the blades.

Pins These must be fine and sharp. Dressmaking pins will do for heavier fabrics, but tiny pins called 'lillikins' or 'lills' are better because they will not damage fine fabrics.

Needles The stitches in patchwork must be as fine and close as you can make them, so choose the finest needle that you can comfortably use. Sizes 9 and 10 are the best.

Thread Traditionally, linen thread was used for joining patches. Linen is still the strongest and best thread to use for knotting or 'tying' the finished patch-work to a backing and interlining, especially if you are making a quilt.

For sewing the patches together you should use a thread that matches the fabric in the patches. Cotton sewing thread, 60 to 80, is ideal for most fabric. Silk thread should be used for fine silk fabrics, but cotton is better for heavier silks, satins and velvets.

Below: It is a good idea to collect together all the tools that you will need before you start preparing your patchwork.

can collect fabrics from a variety of sources: pieces left over from dress-making, the unworn parts of old clothes or short remnants which are sold off in shops relatively cheaply.

You may, however, have a particular colour scheme in mind and so wish to buy all the fabric required, but there is a special satisfaction in knowing that you have made something beautiful and useful for next to nothing.

As patchwork is such a sentimental craft, perhaps you will want to include scraps of special fabric that have a personal significance. This will certainly increase the pleasure you will get from making and using your patch-work. There are a few basic rules, however, that you must observe if your patchwork is to last.

Quality, age and weight

Always use fabric of good quality, whether it is old or new. The best fabrics to use are those which do not fray or stretch and are firm in weave and texture. Good quality cotton, the fabric most commonly used in old patchwork, is still the best material.

Collect enough fabric to complete the design before you start sewing. Handsewn patchwork takes a long time to complete and you may not be able to get hold of the fabric you need later on.

Be careful when mixing different weights. A strong damask patch will put too much strain on a fine fabric stitched next to it and will eventually pull it to pieces.

Patchwork made from fine cotton and corduroy, for example, will be lumpy and will never lie flat. However, if you combine corduroy with suitable fabrics of a similar weight – woollens and tweeds for instance – your patch-work will be successful.

If you want to include old fabric in your patchwork, check it first for worn parts by holding it up to the light, then circle the worn areas with pencil or chalk so that you will avoid them when cutting the patches.

When mixing old and new fabrics, wash the new fabric first to prevent it from shrinking; and of course, check that all fabrics are colourfast.

If you are working with lightweight fabrics or fabrics which are so transparent that the turnings show through, use non-woven interfacing instead of papers and leave it in the finished work. There is no reason why you should not use very delicate lightweight fabric, provided you do not mix the

Above: Leather scraps can be used to make patchwork. The designer of this cushion has used hexagon rosettes in one section and a Sunray design in another, linking them by using the same combination of colours.

Use white thread for joining light colours and black for darker fabrics. A black thread is less obvious than white when joining dark colours to white.

Suitable fabrics

Part of the fun of patchwork is collecting together all the scraps and odds and ends of fabric in the colours and patterns of your choice. Nothing is more stimulating to good patchwork design than a widely varied collection of fabrics in all sorts of shades and textures. Keep a bag or box especially for possible patchwork fabrics. You

weights. A coverlet made from early nineteenth century muslin dress fabrics is still in existence, in quite good condition.

Other fabrics

Man-made fabrics are not really suitable for patchwork as their crease resistant qualities make them too springy to fold accurately over the corners of the papers.

Beware of silk. Do not be tempted by its fine colours and attractive sheen to mix it with cottons. It will wear out much sooner than the cotton and there is nothing more irritating than having to unpick patchwork to repair a patch which has worn badly.

' Silk can look splendid if it is used in patchwork on its own or mixed with satin and velvet, but it should always be of the best quality. Many a once beautiful Victorian silk quilt is in shreds now, while humbler and older cotton quilts are still in good condition.

Velvet will combine well with silk and satin, but it is difficult to handle. The pile tends to 'creep' the patch out of position when sewing. Remember to consider the direction of the pile in each patch.

There are other, more unusual fabrics which can be used in patchwork. One of the oldest pieces in existence is a canopy made of gazelle

Above: Good quality cotton is still a popular fabric for patchwork. It is especially suitable for items like this child's bedspread, which must stand up to heavy wear.

Above: Silk cushions, made up in softly coloured hexagonal shapes that complement the fabric.

Top: With its rich colours and luxurious texture, velvet [velveteen] makes beautiful patchwork. Keep shapes simple, as it is not an easy fabric to work with.

hide, which is now in a Cairo museum. Leather patchwork can look very effective today too and scraps are often sold cheaply in craft shops. They can be made up into bags, cushion covers, wall hangings, bedspreads and clothes. Leather patches do not need turnings, so they can be quickly stitched together by sewing machine.

Felt, although it will not wash or last as long as woven fabrics, comes in many bright colours and can be quickly machine stitched into toys or hangings.

Plastic-coated fabric could also be used for patchwork and can be machine stitched by butting patches together and stitching the raw edges.

Chapter 2
Patchwork techniques

Basic techniques

With the help of a sewing machine bright and colourful patchwork fabric can be constructed in only a fraction of the time it takes to join patches by hand. However, even with the hurried pace of life today many people prefer to make patchwork in the traditional way.

If you are going to make machined patchwork, choose patches 4cm (1½in) or more in length, as smaller patches are best joined by hand. The machine method is particularly suitable for patchwork that is to be made up into clothes. However, whichever method you choose, the patches must be prepared for sewing in the same way.

Preparing the patches

Begin by cutting out the papers. This must be done carefully and accurately as it will affect the final 'fit' of your patchwork. Either cut the papers out two at a time using scissors, holding the template firmly in place on two thicknesses of paper; or use a scalpel or craft knife and cut through several thicknesses of paper at once.

Use the window template to cut the patches from the fabric. They must be cut one at a time with a sharp pair of scissors. Make sure that at least two sides of the template lie along the straight grain of the fabric.

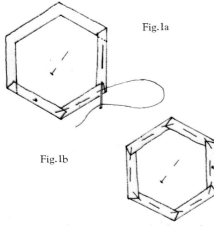

Fig.1a

Fig.1b

The patches must now be basted to the papers. Pin the paper to the wrong side of the fabric patch. Then, fold over the turnings all round and baste them down. Start basting in the middle of one side and work round the patch, taking a stitch to hold down the fold on each corner (figs.1a, 1b).

Take care on the corners as you fold down the double overlap. The material must fit the paper exactly. The sharp points of diamond patches need particular care (figs.2a, 2b, 2c).

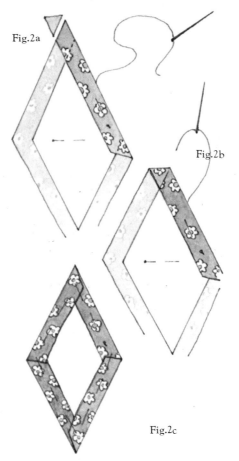

Fig.2a

Fig.2b

Fig.2c

Fine fabrics Silks and some cottons can be permanently marked by pins and basting stitches. To avoid damaging them, do not pin the patch to the paper but hold it in place and stick the edges down with masking tape (fig.3). Baste the corners through the seam allowances only.

Joining patches by hand

Take two patches and place them right sides together. To secure the thread, take a small stitch about 6mm (¼in) from one corner, take the thread to the corner and oversew [overcast] along one side, taking in the thread and the securing stitch (fig.4). The stitches should be fine and close. Push the needle through the fabric at right angles to the edge and take up only two or three threads of fabric with

Opposite: As the patches have been joined, the basting stitches and papers are ready to be removed from this piece of patchwork. The design that has been formed is known as Baby's Blocks.

Figs. 1a, 1b The paper pinned to the wrong side of the patch and the turnings turned in and basted.
Figs. 2a, 2b, 2c Care must be taken when folding down and basting the corners of a patch. The points of diamonds need particular care. Trimming the corners of triangles and diamonds will help to achieve a neat finish.
Fig. 3 Fine fabrics can be taped on to the papers so that pins and basting stitches do not mark them.
Fig. 4 Joining patches by oversewing [overcasting] them together.

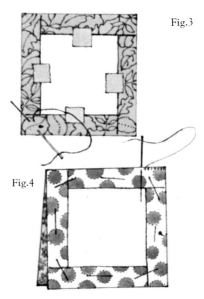

Fig.3

Fig.4

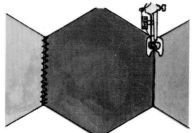

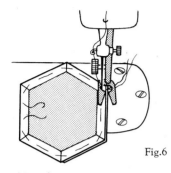

Fig.5

Fig.6

Fig. 5 Non-fraying fabrics can be joined together quickly with machine zigzag stitch. The patches are simply butted together.
Fig. 6 Fraying fabrics can be joined too by machine zigzag stitch. The patches are placed right sides together beneath the presser foot.
Fig. 7 A long length of thread should be left at each end of the seam.
Fig. 8 A completed piece of machined patchwork.

each stitch. Do not sew through the paper.

To finish the seam, sew back for three or four stitches and cut the thread. Flatten the seam and continue sewing the other patches together by making up groups or units.

Joining patches by machine

Square and rectangular patches can easily be joined together with a straight stitch machine (see page 32). Other shapes may also be sewn together by folding down the turnings and sewing along the seam line with a straight stitch machine, but it is difficult to make accurate patchwork this way. By using a swing needle sewing machine with zigzag stitch you can accurately join patches of any shape together. Leather, suede, felt and plastic-coated fabrics are particularly simple to join with a swing needle machine as they do not fray. Simply butt the patches together and zigzag over the edges (fig.5).

Preparing the machine You need no special equipment or attachments for machined patchwork. Use a medium sized needle, a No.14 (Continental No.90) and change it more often than normal as the patchwork papers tend to blunt the point. The sewing thread will be more obvious on the finished patchwork than it is on handsewn patches so choose the colour carefully. White thread looks good with mixed colours, or you could pick out one of the main colours in the patchwork. The thread should be fine, No.50 or 60. Use a mercerized cotton or a synthetic thread according to the fabric.

Loosen the top tension slightly and select a stitch width, or 'swing', of $1\frac{1}{2}$ to 2. Use a medium stitch length. Experiment first with folded scraps of fabric.

You will need to adjust the stitch length slightly according to the size of the patch. A patch with 7.5cm (3in) sides will need a slightly longer stitch than one with 5cm (2in) sides, although the stitch width will be the same for both.

Machining the patches together Prepare the patches in exactly the same way as you would for hand sewing. If the patchwork is intended for fashion appliqué, use non-woven interfacing instead of papers and leave them in the finished work. To join two fraying fabric patches, place them right sides together beneath the presser foot (fig.6). They should match evenly

at the corners, but allow the lower patch to show very slightly along the working edge so that you can check that the stitches are penetrating both patches.

A swing needle swings from left to right and back again. Left is the starting point and you must always start with the needle ready to swing to the left.

Turn the balance wheel manually towards you so that the needle pierces the top right hand corner of both patches. Lower the presser foot and stitch slowly along the edge. At the left hand swing the needle should pierce the fabric and papers of the two patches. At the right hand swing it should pass just beyond the edges of the patches.

When you reach the end of the working edge the needle should swing to the right for the last stitch. You will then be ready to swing the needle back to the starting point on the next seam. Give the balance wheel a half turn towards you, lift the presser foot and remove the patches, leaving at least 5cm (2in) of thread before cutting off (fig.7). The long ends are essential as they must be tied off to secure the stitching. Tie the thread in a double knot as you complete each seam.

Fig.7

Fig.8

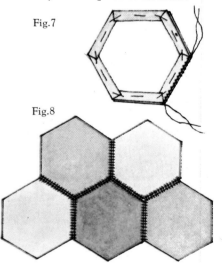

It may be necessary to help the machine over the corners with some densely woven fabrics, or with acutely angled shapes like diamonds, as there may be up to eight layers of fabric for the needle to penetrate.

When you open out the seams you will see that the patches are joined together with firm even stitches (fig.8), straight on the front and criss-crossed on the back. Add as many patches as you need, working through the whole piece of patchwork or joining the patches together in groups as you would for hand sewn patchwork.

Finishing off

When all the patches have been joined together, press the patchwork on the wrong side with a warm iron. If you have included velvet, be sure to press over a needle board or a thick towel. If you wish to press the work on the right side, take out the basting stitches first to prevent them marking the fabric. Straighten the edges by adding half patches. Then remove basting threads and papers.

Mounting

Patchwork intended for appliqué must be mounted to the base fabric. If you have used non-woven interfacing instead of papers, leave it in. Baste around the edges of the patchwork to hold the turnings in place.

Give the patchwork a good press on the wrong side. Pin and baste it into place on the base fabric and sew down with tiny hem stitches. If the area of patchwork is large, catch it to the base fabric occasionally.

Lining

Whether sewn by hand or machine, patchwork makes a strong fabric. But unless it is used for appliqué, patchwork should always be lined, because the grain of the patches does not always run in the same direction and the work is easily distorted. Use firmly woven cotton or a similar fabric for the lining. It can be attached to the patchwork in a variety of ways.

The edges of the patchwork can be bound with lining. The lining should be 2.5cm (1in) larger all round than the patchwork. Turn in the edges of the lining 6mm ($\frac{1}{4}$in) all around it. Baste and press the edges.

Lay the patchwork on top of the

Fig.9

Fig.10

lining, wrong sides together. Fold down the surrounding lining fabric onto the right side of the patchwork, making a neat mitre at each corner (fig.9). Baste the edges in place. Slip stitch the mitre and slip stitch or machine the edges (fig.10). If the patchwork is fairly large, catch it to the lining at regular intervals.

Alternatively, the lining and patchwork can be bagged. The lining should be 6mm-9mm ($\frac{1}{4}$in-$\frac{3}{8}$in) (or the width of the patchwork turnings) larger all round than the patchwork. Unfold the turnings on the edge of the patchwork. Place the lining and the patchwork right sides together, baste around three sides and part of the fourth, the width of the patch turnings from the edge. Machine or hand sew along the line of basting stitches. Clip the corners then turn the 'bag' right side out and slip stitch the opening. Make a line of running stitches all round the 'bag' 3mm ($\frac{1}{8}$in) from the edges to hold them firm. Catch the patchwork to the lining if necessary.

Patchwork can also be finished with piping, bound with bias strips, or the edges of the patchwork and lining can be turned in and the lining oversewn [overcast] to the patchwork.

Interlining

If the work is to be made into a bedcover, interlining should be placed between patchwork and lining. Synthetic wadding [batting] is the ideal material. It is washable, quick drying and available in a variety of weights.

Lay a piece of lining fabric, 5cm (2in) larger all round than the patchwork, wrong side up on a large flat surface. Place the wadding on top and the patchwork, right side up, on top of the wadding.

Baste the three layers together with regular parallel lines of stitching worked from side to side and from top to bottom. It is important that all the lines of basting which are parallel to each other are worked in the same direction to avoid wrinkles (fig.11).

Work knots through all the thicknesses at regular intervals across the whole piece of work (fig.12). The knots should be made on the lining side.

Bind the edges of the patchwork with lining as described above, or trim the lining 6mm-9mm ($\frac{1}{4}$in-$\frac{3}{8}$in) larger all round than the patchwork, unfold the patchwork turnings and finish off the edges in one of the other ways mentioned. Then, remove all the basting stitches from the work.

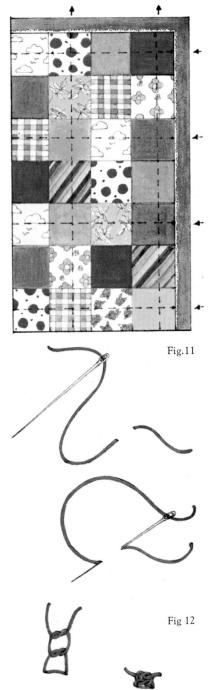

Fig.11

Fig 12

Fig. 9 Folding and trimming the corner of the lining for mitring.
Fig.10 The lining slip stitched in place on the right side.
Fig.11 Patchwork sewn to lining and interlining with lines of basting stitches, worked from side to side and from top to bottom.
Fig. 12 The knotting technique used to hold the layers of lining, interlining and patchwork together.

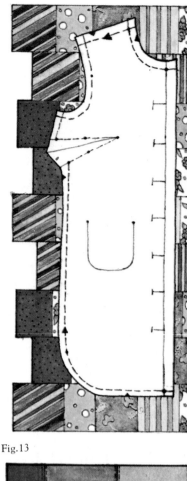

Fig.13

Fig.14

Fig. 13 A pattern positioned on a piece of cut and stagger patchwork, which has been made up to accomodate the pattern.
Fig. 14 Patchwork fabric will have extra strength if it is topstitched.

Above right: The simple lines of this blouse make it an ideal style for machine worked patchwork.

Dressmaking with patchwork

To make clothes from hand sewn or machine patchwork, choose a fairly simple pattern. Spread out all the pattern pieces, leaving those for facings to one side – these should be cut from the lining fabric rather than the patchwork.

You must make sure that the shapes will fit well together at the seams, allowing for turnings. So before you begin making the patchwork draw the pattern of the patches onto your paper pattern. Use a felt tip pen to avoid tearing the pattern.

Make a duplicate pattern of the garment on stiff paper, marking both shapes and colour. Cut out these stiff shapes and use them as papers for the patches. Mark the original pattern and the papers so that you have a guide which will enable you to stitch the patches together in the right sequence.

You can use this method for hand or machine sewn patches, although it is particularly useful if you are joining patches by hand, as you only sew together the exact number of patches you require.

If you wish you can construct a length of fabric from machine sewn patches and lay the pattern pieces out on it as on ordinary fabric (fig.13).

Hand and machine sewn patchwork must be lined. Baste the lining to the patchwork and use them as one fabric, making up the pattern according to the manufacturer's instructions. Use lining fabric for the facings.

The patchwork fabric will be given extra strength if you top stitch the garment you are making (fig.14).

American block construction

The block method of patchwork construction needs to be explained in this chapter as it is a technique of joining patches. It is the most common type of patchwork design in America. It developed in the nineteenth century and was greatly aided by the invention of the sewing machine about 1850.

Basically, the block method consists of piecing patches into a square to form one pattern unit or block. When enough blocks have been made to form a quilt, they are sewn or 'set' together; either directly adjacent to each other, or separated by strips or blocks of plain fabric.

The block method greatly reduces sewing time as papers are not necessary, and the straight seams involved lend themselves especially well to machine sewing, if you choose to join your patches in this way.

The method also gives enormous scope for design and invention. There are two stages of design – that of the blocks themselves and the final arrangement of the blocks.

Building blocks
Blocks can be any size, from 15cm

Below: A quilt constructed by the American block method. This pattern is made up of Winged Square blocks.

Fig. 1a Four groups of two triangles sewn together – the first stage in the construction of a four-patch Windmill block.

Fig. 1b The squares joined in pairs.

Fig. 1c One complete square patch.

Fig. 1d The completed four-patch block.

Fig. 2 Basic nine-patch block.

Fig. 3 Old Maid's Puzzle (four-patch).

Fig. 4 Bear's Tracks or Bear's Paw (four-patch).

Fig. 5 Diagonal lattice strips separating blocks.

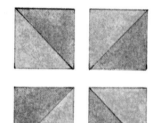

Fig.1a

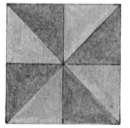

Fig.1b

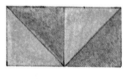

Fig.1c

Fig.1d

(6in) to 60cm (24in) square. The most common, and the most manageable, sizes are 25cm (10in) and 30cm (12in) square.

Despite the speed with which blocks can be pieced on the sewing machine, accuracy, as with all forms of patchwork, is of the utmost importance. The secret of success is to use window templates, allowing 6mm ($\frac{1}{4}$in) for seams. Cut out the fabric around the outside of the template and on the wrong side, pencil along the inner border of the template. The pencil line will act as a seam guide.

A general rule when piecing a block is to join any triangles first to form squares, and then to build up the squares to form bigger and bigger units. A good example of this is the construction of the Windmill block (figs.1a-1d).

It is a good idea to pin the points at which the seams meet as you work, to ensure that the lines of the pattern match. Open up and press seams flat as you finish sewing each one. Spraying the assembled patches lightly with spray starch is a quick and efficient way of obtaining flat units.

Most pieced blocks belong either to the 4-patch or to the 9-patch family (see examples below). They involve either four or nine basic units, which can be sub-divided in any number of ways.

Setting

The final patchwork design depends on the arrangement of the individual blocks. Joining the blocks is known as 'setting'. Blocks can be joined side by side to create an unbroken pattern over the whole surface of the patchwork. Windmill and Broken Dishes are particularly attractive set this way for a repetitive unbroken result. However, many patterns can look messy if set in this way. To separate the blocks and throw each pattern into relief, it is often best to set each pieced block beside a square of plain material to create a chequered effect.

Another way is to alternate patterned and plain squares diagonally, using half-squares at the edges.

Pieced blocks can also be set with lattice bands, usually about 8cm (3in) wide excluding seams, which separate and frame each block (fig.4). This is sometimes known as sash work. Lattice strips, cut on the straight grain, can also be set diagonally, again using half-blocks at the sides (fig.5).

Fig. 2

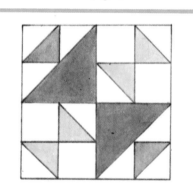

Fig. 3

Fig. 4

Chapter 3
Patchwork shapes

Squares & rectangles

Old patchwork made entirely from squares is rare. Grandmother's Postage Stamp, in which the colours run diagonally across the patchwork, is one of the few traditional patterns made up entirely of squares. All-over patterns made from the same repeated unit are known as one-patch designs.

Many beautiful and complex design are based on the square, as it is a shape which can be divided up in a variety of ways. The Windmill design is one example, as the squares are divided diagonally into triangles. In the Roman Square pattern the squares are divided into three rectangular strips.

The rectangle too is rarely used as a shape on its own. The two traditional designs based on it are the zigzag and brick-wall patterns. Rectangles traditionally were often used for bordering quilts and coverlets.

The finished effect of your patchwork will depend on the combinations of colours you choose and where you place them in relation to each other. The Hit and Miss design, shown in our photograph, is made up of four-patch blocks using alternating light and dark fabrics.

Intricate patterns can be made by joining squares and rectangles diagonally. These sort of patterns are best joined by hand. These two shapes are also effective used as borders, particularly on a plain background.

Squares and rectangles, however, can be used on their own to make simple and effective patchwork. Beginners to patchwork would find articles such as the baby's quilt, or a cushion made by the cut-and-stagger technique, ideal practice-ground for using these shapes before progressing to using them in block patterns (see page 29).

Joining squares and rectangles

By hand Squares and rectangles can be joined by the traditional hand-sewing technique described in Chapter 2. Alternatively, you can join your patches without using papers. Cut out the patches, then take two and, with right sides facing, join them carefully with a small running stitch (fig.1).

Join the patches into strips, making sure that the seams are all the same width. Press the seam allowances together to one side and join the strips together. Do not press the seams open as in the oversewing [overcasting] and machine methods, as this will put too much strain on the running stitch and may weaken the seams.

By machine Squares and rectangles can be machined together using the swing-needle machine methods explained in Chapter 2. They can also be joined quickly and simply by seaming them on a straight stitch machine, as described here.

When you have decided on the size of your patches, cut them out carefully, following the straight grain of the fabric, or use a template. Provided you have been absolutely accurate in cutting out each patch, then all you need to do is stitch the patches together in long strips (fig.2). Use the foot of the machine as a guide to ensure that you take exactly the same

Fig. 1 Sewing squares together by hand with running stitches.
Fig. 2 Sewing squares together into a long strip using machine running stitch.

Opposite, above: A quilt made up entirely of squares, which have been used as diamond shapes. The pastel centre of the quilt darkens gradually to a plain red border.

Opposite, below left: A quilt with Hit and Miss four-patch blocks joined by strips of dark and light blue fabric.

Opposite, below right: Rectangles, cut from contrasting shades of wool, are stitched together to make diagonal zigzag shapes.

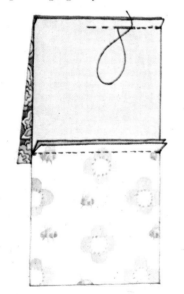

Fig.1

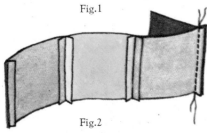

Fig.2

Right: A baby's cot quilt made up of hand sewn squares in an all-over design.

Below: Rectangles arranged in a 'brick wall' pattern.

Bottom: A border of diagonally-arranged squares.

allowance on each seam. Press the seams flat and sew the strips together.

Cut-and-stagger technique

Another way of joining squares or rectangles by machine is the cut-and-stagger technique (figs.3, 4, 5). It is extremely quick and easy to do, although the distribution of colour and design is fairly limited.

Take strips of material of equal length and of equal or varying width and machine them together, right sides facing, taking 9mm (⅜in) seams. The number and width of the strips, and their length, will be determined by the size of the patchwork required.

Press open the seams, then cut across the fabric at intervals, in straight lines, allowing for seams on each side of the cutting line.

The resulting strips can be rearranged in a variety of ways and machined together to form patchwork fabric with a random pattern.

The cut-and-stagger technique is also suitable for dressmaking, as described on page 28.

Making templates

To draw a square Using a protractor, draw a right angle. Then, set the span of a pair of compasses to the length of the square. Put the pin at the right angle and draw arcs to cut both arms of the right angle. With the same span, put the pin at the points where the arcs cut the lines and draw two more arcs. The point at which these intersect becomes the fourth corner of the square (fig.6).

To draw a rectangle Using a protractor, draw a right angle. Using compasses mark off the two sides by intersecting the arms. Draw arcs from these intersections, setting the span of the compasses to the length of the other side. The point at which the arcs intersect forms the fourth corner of the rectangle (fig.7).

Fig. 3 The first stage of making a piece of cut and stagger patchwork. Strips are cut and arranged horizontally.
Fig. 4 The strips are sewn together, then cut vertically ready for staggering.
Fig.5 A completed piece of cut-and-stagger patchwork.
Figs. 6, 7 Constructing a square and a rectangle.

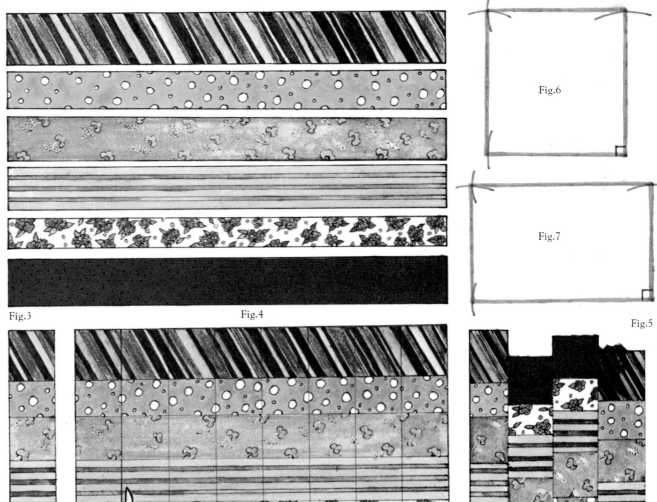

Fig.3

Fig.4

Fig.5

Fig.6

Fig.7

Triangles & diamonds

Triangles and diamonds have always been popular shapes for patchwork, whether used alone or combined with others. This is because the triangle is easy to form by folding a square diagonally and then cutting it. It is also a particularly useful shape for using up very small scraps of fabric.

The bold angular shape of the diamond can be used for many beautiful patchwork designs. However, it is rather a tricky shape for beginners to use because the acute angles at the points make it difficult to fold the fabric neatly. For this reason the diamond was a favourite among American women for making best or Masterpiece quilts. The cutting and piecing of the patches was such an exacting process that the work was begun only when enough quilts had been made for daily use and when the worker would not have to rush the work.

Many Masterpiece quilts survive today because they were usually laid on the bed in the guest room and so received little wear.

Triangles

There are two kinds of triangle used in patchwork, the pyramid and the long triangle.

The pyramid, also known as the half-diamond, has a short base line with the two other sides equal in length. The shape can be made by halving a diamond widthways.

A strip of intersecting light and dark pyramids is called Dog's Tooth, and this design can be used as a border pattern or the strips can be sewn

Far left: A modern quilt in which the basic block is a dark blue square. Two triangles (one red and one multi-coloured) and a yellow trapezoid have been sewn onto each individual block. The way in which the blocks are stitched together forms the design.

Left: Saw Tooth Star, a four-patch design, which combines triangles and squares.

Fig.1

Fig.2

Fig. 1 An overall one-patch design, known as A Thousand Pyramids.
Fig. 2 Alternating light and dark coloured vertical bands form a design known as Streak of Lightning.

Right: A tablecloth with multi-coloured long triangles alternating with plain white triangles.

together to make a one-patch design called A Thousand Pyramids (fig.1).

Vertical bands alternating light and dark colours form the Streak of Lightning design (fig.2). Another interesting strip design is called Flying Geese, and there is a block design, Wild Goose Chase, that uses the same structure. As a single block the latter makes an excellent bold design for a cushion cover.

The long triangle has a base line longer than the two equal sides. It is most commonly made by dividing a square diagonally, but it can also be made by halving a diamond lengthways.

Cotton Reels (fig.3) is a design popular for borders and all-over patterns. By combining half-square triangles with quarter-square triangles and squares, as in Whirlwind (fig.4),

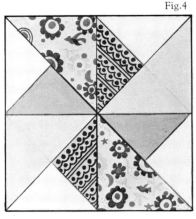

Fig.3

Fig.4

Fig. 3 The Cotton Reel design, popular for borders and all-over patterns.
Fig. 4 Whirlwind, a design which combines half-square triangles with quarter-square triangles and squares.

Left, above: A quilt and bolster in a block design known as Jacob's Ladder.

Left, below: A detail of a Shoo-fly design bedspread, in which triangles and squares are combined in each block.

for example, an almost infinite variety of patterns can be formed. Star patterns like the Saw Tooth Star and the Rising Star are popular for quilt blocks.

A number of designs are formed by half-square triangles grouped to run diagonally across a square block. The words 'road', 'trial' or 'ladder' are included in their names, due to the effect of the pattern formed. Jacob's Ladder, a pre-Revolutionary American design, is one example. Its name changed to The Road to California as settlers moved westwards.

Natural objects are also represented using the half-square triangle. Maple Leaf and Pine Tree are two American favourites. The Shoo-fly design, named after a wild plant, also uses this shape.

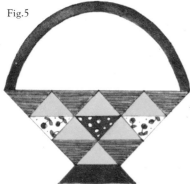

Fig.5

Fig. 5 The Basket design is made up of long triangles, which are joined together, then appliquéd to a plain background.

Above: The long diamond is one of the main shapes used in this Basket of Scraps design.

Right: The Baby Blocks pattern is formed by lozenge diamonds placed in groups of three. One fabric forms the 'lid' while another two form the 'sides'.

The Basket is a traditional pattern found on both sides of the Atlantic. The completed basket is usually applied, with a handle, to a background fabric (fig.5). Sometimes basket quilts were made with a different flower applied in each basket.

Diamonds

Again, there are two variations of the diamond shape, the lozenge and the long diamond.

The lozenge is made up of two equilateral triangles and can be formed by dividing a hexagon, so it therefore combines well with the latter shape. Six lozenges can form a six-point star (fig.6), which can then be adapted to a hexagon if six more lozenges are slotted in around the outside edges of it. Six-point stars, linked together by single diamonds, will form an attractive appliqué border pattern.

The Box or Baby's Blocks pattern is also made from lozenges. With carefully chosen colours it can create a vivid optical illusion.

The long diamond makes an eight-point star. This is known as the Lemoine Star. The Virginia Star, with four diamonds in each arm, is an extension of the basic eight-point and the splendid Star of Bethlehem a further extension. The colours in the Star of Bethlehem need very careful planning to achieve the right effect.

Making templates and patches

To draw a pyramid or half diamond. This shape is an isosceles triangle (fig.7). Draw a straight line AB which will be the base, and set the span of the compasses to the length of the proposed two equal sides. With the point of the compasses at A and B in turn, draw two arcs to intersect at C. Join AC and BC to form the triangle.

To draw a long triangle The long triangle can be constructed in the same way as a pyramid, but it is most commonly made by dividing a square diagonally.

To draw a lozenge This shape is formed by drawing two equilateral

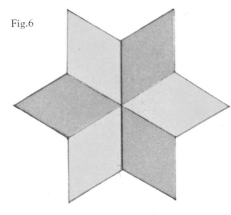

Fig.6

triangles and setting them base to base (fig.8). The equilateral triangle has three equal sides. Set the span of the compasses to the measurement AB when drawing the arcs. Construct in the same way as the isosceles triangle.

To draw a long diamond Before drawing, decide on the length of the sides. Draw a line AB to this length (fig.9). Place a protractor at B and mark 45° with a dot, C. Draw a line from B to C. Set the compasses to the length AB. With the point of the compasses on B, mark the length on BC at E. With the point at E and then at A, mark the arcs to cross at F. Join EF and AF. Finally, check the accuracy of your work by making sure that the angles FEB and FAB are 135° and that AFE and ABE are 45°.

Making patches

When cutting triangular patches make sure that one edge follows the straight grain of the fabric. When cutting diamonds, two edges or one of the axes should be on the grain. You will find it helpful at first to use a slightly heavier paper than normal for diamond patches. This will make it easier to feel the points as you fold the fabric in place over the patch.

Fig. 6 A six-point star, formed by joining lozenge shapes.
Fig. 7 Constructing an isosceles triangle (pyramid or half diamond).
Fig. 8 Constructing a lozenge shape.
Fig. 9 Constructing a long diamond.

Below left: The Star of Bethlehem design, which is constructed by joining long diamonds.

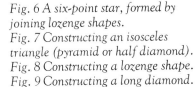

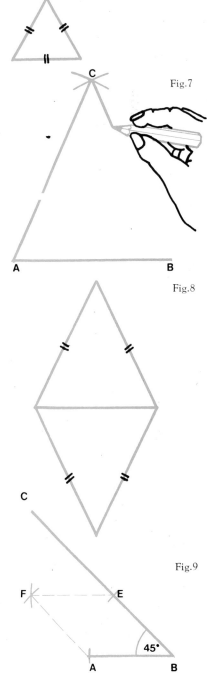

Fig.7

Fig.8

Fig.9

Hexagons or honeycombs

The hexagon, or honeycomb, is probably the best known and most loved of patchwork shapes. It is very simple to use, and the wide angles at the corners mean that there is no difficulty in making a neat fold over the paper. Hexagons are regular shapes which, like triangles, squares and rectangles, can be joined to form a solid pattern or one-patch design.

The rosette

Seven hexagons sewn together form a rosette. This is a good basic shape and

Right: A Grandmother's Flower Garden quilt. Double rosettes are joined to plain white hexagons in this popular, traditional design.

patchwork can be made entirely of rosettes. Colours should be carefully planned, however, or the patchwork will be a jumble of colours and no regular pattern will emerge. Each central hexagon should be surrounded by six patches. The latter should be all the same colour. The window template is a help in choosing which part of a patterned fabric is to appear on each patch.

A group of single rosettes can be linked quite simply by making the central patches of the same colour.

A second row of hexagons in another tone or colour make a double rosette and yet another row of patches makes a triple rosette.

The 'Grandmother's Flower Garden' design is one of the prettiest and most popular ways of using double rosettes. The design is also sometimes called 'French Bouquet'. A central patch of plain fabric is surrounded by patches cut from a floral print. The second row is cut from a plain or patterned green fabric. This gives the effect of a large bright flower surrounded by foliage.

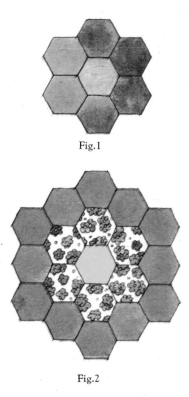

Fig.1

Fig.2

The double rosettes are linked by plain white hexagons which represent paths meandering among flowerbeds.

You can make up the whole patchwork fabric in this way, or you could simply make up double rosettes and apply them to a plain white background fabric. This would be an ideal way to make yourself a pretty, old-fashioned bedspread. Single or double rosettes are such a simple and attractive form of decoration that you could also apply them to clothes at random, as border decorations or as pockets. They could also brighten furnishings like table cloths, mats and napkins, curtains or cushion covers.

Other hexagon designs

There are many variations on the basic rosette. It can be enlarged into a six-point star to make an attractive design for a cushion cover or a spectacular centre piece for a table cloth or quilt.

Hexagon patterns make attractive border designs as well. Ocean Waves is an old pattern that has edged many a quilt. The waves can be as deep or as wide as you like. The colours should be carefully chosen to shade from light to dark to get the best effect. Festoons and Garlands also make attractive borders.

All the designs illustrated can be applied or worked as part of the whole patchwork fabric, except for the Festoon which must always be applied to a background fabric.

The coffin and church window are both variations on the honeycomb hexagon formed by elongating the basic shape. They are not as popular as the regular hexagon, but can be made into attractive patchwork, either on their own or combined with other shapes. Church windows, for instance, combine well with squares, octagons and rectangles (see page 49).

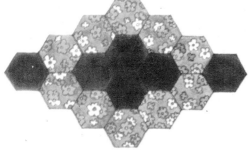

Fig.3

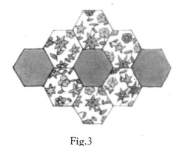

Fig.4

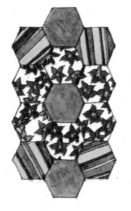

Fig.5

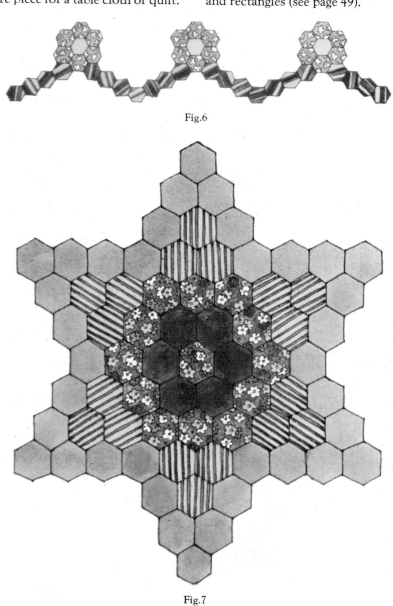

Fig.6

Fig.7

44

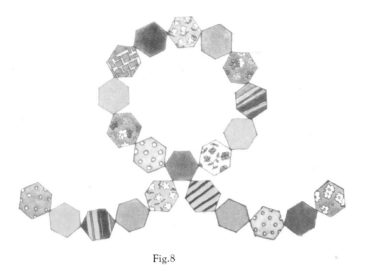

Fig.8

Fig.9

Fig.10a

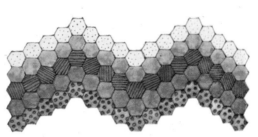

Fig.10b

Fig.11

Fig. 1 Single rosette.
Fig. 2 Double rosette.
Fig. 3 Diamond rosette.
Fig. 4 Elongated rosette.
Fig. 5 Developed rosette.
Fig. 6 Garland.
Fig. 7 Six-point star.
Fig. 8 Honeycomb patches
appliquéd in a Festoon.
Fig. 9 Double rosette with three
different colours in the inner one.
Figs. 10a, 10b. Two ways of
forming the Ocean Waves design.
Fig. 11 Church window border

Left: The single rosette, star centre piece and Ocean Waves border in this quilt reveal the variety of ways hexagons and colours can be linked to form beautiful patterns.

45

Fig.12

Fig. 12 Constructing a hexagon.

Below: The subtle off-centre shading of light and dark colours in this quilt has been carefully planned. A patterned fabric has been used for the single rosettes and creates an almost kaleidoscopic effect.

Making templates

To draw hexagons Hexagons can be formed from circles, as the six sides of a hexagon are equal in length to the radius of a circle. Draw a circle with compasses and mark off a point anywhere on the circle. Then without altering the span, place the pin on that point and intersect the circle. Place the pin on that point and mark off another point. Repeat this three times more and then join up the points to form a hexagon (fig.12).

Other shapes & combinations

Pentagons

With its five equal sides and angles, the pentagon can never be used alone for patchwork as it will not lie flat. Twelve equilateral pentagons, however, will form a ball (fig.1). Pin cushions made in this way from velvet were popular with the Victorians.

Pentagon balls can be made into attractive presents today. You can make them in pretty cottons, fill them with lavender or pot-pourri and hang them in a wardrobe.

Large balls made of brightly coloured felt are an ideal gift for a baby. The felt patches need no turnings and they can be sewn together with a decorative embroidery stitch like feather stitch.

The adapted pentagon, made from a lozenge diamond with one point cut off, is a much more popular patchwork shape than the equilateral pentagon. It is often combined with hexagons and lozenge diamonds to make the Box and Star design.

If the base of the pentagon is the same length as the sides of the hexagon, it forms an attractive star pattern. The spaces between the points can either be filled in with lozenge diamonds to make a large overall hexagon shape, or they can be filled in with larger hexagons.

Making templates

You will probably have to make your own templates for these more unusual shapes. To make an adapted pentagon, simply draw a lozenge diamond (see page 41), and cut off one end so that the base is the length you require.

An equilateral pentagon is simple to draw within a circle (fig.2). Draw a line from the centre of the circle to the edge. Measure an angle of 72° and extend this to the circumference. Repeat four times and join up the five points to form the pentagon.

Fig.2

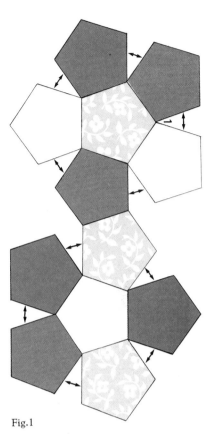

Fig.1

Fig. 1 An assembly guide for a pentagon ball.
Fig. 2 Constructing an equilateral pentagon.

Left: Pentagons cannot be used alone for patchwork as they will not lie flat when joined. However, they can be made up into a ball which can be filled with lavender.

Octagons

The octagon is a much more popular shape than the pentagon. Although it cannot be used alone, with its eight wide angles it is an even easier shape to use than the hexagon. It combines well with many shapes – squares, rectangles, triangles and church window hexagons.

Dutch Tile is one of the simplest all-over designs to make. The patchwork really does look like pretty Dutch tiles if you join octagons of blue print fabric with small squares of plain blue.

An octagon becomes a square if triangles are added to the four slanting sides.

Making templates

You can construct an octagon within a circle in exactly the same way as a pentagon (fig.2). The angle at the centre is 45°.

Rhomboids

The rhomboid is a parallelogram adapted from a rectangle. It is useful as a fill-in shape and can be combined with a variety of other shapes. It is most commonly used to create designs with perspective. The simplest is the traditional border pattern, where rhomboids are sewn together in pairs of alternatively light and dark shades to give a pleated effect. Triangles can be added to make a strip of patchwork.

Fig.3

Below: Irregular geometric shapes can be sewn together to make striking designs.

Fig. 3 Honeycombs and lozenge diamonds combined.

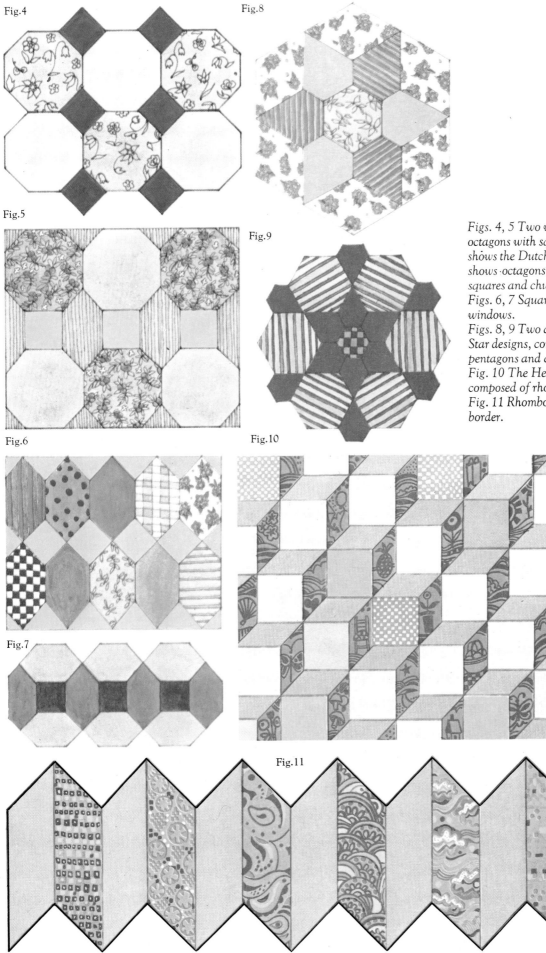

Fig.4

Fig.8

Fig.5

Fig.9

Figs. 4, 5 Two ways of using octagons with squares. Fig. 4 shows the Dutch Tile design. Fig. 5 shows octagons joined with squares and church windows.
Figs. 6, 7 Squares and church windows.
Figs. 8, 9 Two different Box and Star designs, combining hexagons, pentagons and diamonds.
Fig. 10 The Heavenly Steps pattern, composed of rhomboids and squares.
Fig. 11 Rhomboids in a pleated border.

Fig.6

Fig.7

Fig.10

Fig.11

Again, if rhomboids of dark and light shades are sewn together in pairs and four pairs are sewn into a star shape, you can make a square block by adding triangles all round.

Rhomboids are also combined with squares in the pattern called Heavenly Steps or Pandora's Box. Like the Baby's Blocks pattern using lozenge diamonds, this is another way of creating an illusion of cubes.

Other quadrilaterals

The trapezium [trapezoid] is another useful fill-in shape that can be combined with a variety of others. The designer of the quilt on page 37 has used it successfully. It is also used in the Secret Drawer pattern with squares, triangles and adapted pentagons.

Adapted rectangles The strip or extended rectangle is a fill-in shape that can be combined in a variety of ways, but the more oddly-shaped adapted rectangle, with one slanting end is more useful. This shape can combined with squares to make a trellis design, or it can be used with squares and octagons to create a basket weave effect. This pattern would need to cover a fairly large area for the pattern to emerge.

Combining shapes

If you enjoy creating your own designs, you can work out many more combinations of all the different shapes. To help you plan the com-

Below: These patchwork cushions show how, with carefully chosen colours, simple shapes can be successfully combined.

binations, you can cut out a number of papers in each shape and move them around like jigsaw pieces until you find a design you like. If you use coloured paper and paper cut from magazines, you will also be able to work out colour relationships as you move the shapes around.

You can create a completely original random patchwork design. On a sheet of drawing paper the same size as your intended finished patchwork, start by drawing in one shape, then work out to the edges, drawing in other random shapes. When you have a design you like, make a key showing how the shapes fit together. Then cut up the original drawing and use the pieces as papers for the patches.

Fig 12

Fig. 12 A detail from a quilt. Six-point stars of lozenge diamonds are combined with hexagons.

Figs. 13-17 Some of the more unusual patchwork shapes. A protractor and compasses will be needed to construct them. The adapted pentagon is constructed by drawing a lozenge diamond (see page 41) and 'cutting off' one point.
Fig. 13 The extended rectangle.
Fig. 14 The adapted rectangle.
Fig. 15 The trapezium [trapezoid].
Fig. 16 The rhomboid.
Fig. 17 The adapted pentagon.

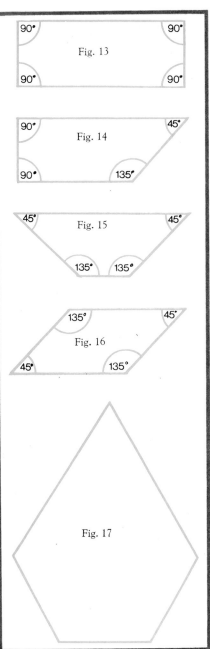

Shell or Clamshell

Shell, or Clamshell, patchwork evolved from a shape that had been used in quilting and embroidery for hundreds of years. It is more tricky to do than other types of patchwork as the shape is difficult to work with. For this reason this kind of patchwork was not popular for many years.

Quite recently, with the surge of interest in this needle art generally, shell patchwork has become popular. It is particularly suitable for making small articles and as appliqué decorations on clothes, because only a small amount of patchwork needs to be made up. The round scalloped edges are attractive as a finish on wide

sleeves, hems, bodices and pockets.

The shell shape is always used on its own as it will not combine with other shapes. The patches, which are shaped like mushrooms, can be sewn together in two different ways; the first creates an all-over type of meandering pattern and the second forms rows, creating the more familiar Fish-scale pattern.

It is easier to use bought, rather than home-made, templates for shell patchwork as it is extremely difficult to cut

the curves accurately. A window template is essential for both the methods of preparing patches. These are described on the next page.

Meandering Shell pattern

In this method the fabric is basted all around the papers (in the same way as for all the other shapes), although the turnings around the lower concave curves should be clipped first. The half-circle edges are then butted together in pairs to create an all-over meandering effect (fig.1).

Fig.1

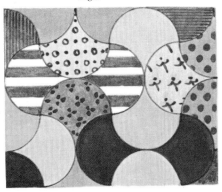

Fish-scale pattern

The more traditional Fish-scale pattern of scallops is one of the most difficult types of patchwork to do. It requires great dexterity and patience to achieve smooth curves, although the resulting scalloped pattern is attractive and well worth the trouble.

In this method the papers are used only as a guide and only the semicircle at the top of the patch is turned under. The patches are arranged in rows with the curved edges overlapping the stems of the previous row (fig.2).

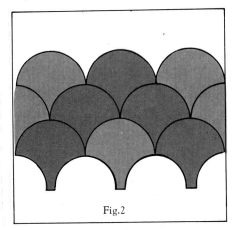

Fig.2

To help achieve smooth curves, you should be even more selective in your choice of fabric than for other shapes. It must be firmly woven, yet fine and soft. Cotton dress fabrics are best.

Far left: The delicate effect of Shell patchwork makes it an ideal trimming for clothes.

Fig. 1 The Meandering Shell pattern, in which the half-circle edges are butted together.
Fig. 2 The Fish-scale pattern, in which the patches are arranged in rows, with the curved stems overlapping the stems of the previous row.

53

Because so much preliminary pinning and basting is done, avoid any fabrics which will be permanently marked.

Shell patchwork looks best in clearly defined straight or diagonal rows or waves, so choose your colours and patterns carefully.

As well as all the usual tools and materials, you will need a base into which pins can be stuck. The patches are laid in straight rows on this. A cork bath mat or piece of insulation board is best.

Method of working

The grain of the fabric should run vertically and horizontally from top to bottom and from side to side of the Shell or Clamshell patch.

There are two ways of preparing Clamshell patches. Both methods require that the convex edge of each patch is hemmed. The two concave edges are left unhemmed, as they will be covered by the next row of patches.

Method 1 This method uses a lining fabric, which is sewn to the patches, and obviously results in heavier, bulkier work than Method 2. It should therefore only be used for articles that will benefit from this extra weight.

Place the window template on the right side of the fabric and trace lightly along the outer line. Cut out the patch using this outline. Then, on the wrong side of the patch, trace the inner line of the template. This will help in placing the lining centrally over the patch. Cut out enough patches to complete two rows of the work.

Using the smaller, solid metal template, cut out a number of shapes in lining fabric. Pin the lining patch centrally to the wrong side of the patch. Then, with the lining uppermost, turn the seam allowance of the patch along the convex edge on to the lining, so that the new curve of the patch matches the outline of the lining exactly.

Baste the hem with small stitches, taking in the fullness of the hem with small regular pleats, to achieve a smooth unbroken curve (fig.3). The basting stitches should go through the lining fabric, but they should not go through to the right side of the patch, as they will remain in the finished work. Remove the pins as you complete each patch.

Method 2 This method uses card patterns which are later removed. Cut a number of card patterns following the outline of the solid template. The card used should be fairly flexible —about the thickness of a postcard. You do not need to cut as many cards as patches since they can be re-used.

Cut out the patches in the same way as for Method 1, but this time marking the guideline on the right side of the fabric. Cut enough to complete two rows.

Pin a card pattern to the centre of a patch on the right side of the fabric, following the guideline (fig.4).

Holding the patch and card with the wrong side of the fabric uppermost, turn the seam allowance to the wrong side of the fabric along the convex curve, following the outline of the pattern as a guide. The hemmed edge should lie exactly level with the edge of the card.

Baste the hem, taking in the fullness of the fabric with small regular pleats (fig.5) as in Method 1, but do not sew the patch to the card. Unpin and remove the card pattern and repeat the process until enough patches have been prepared to complete two rows of work.

Assembly

The patches are joined in the same way whichever method was used for hemming.

Lay the first row of patches on the board. Following fig.6 arrange the patches so that the sides of each patch are just touching and the tops of the convex curves lie in a straight line. Lay them against a ruler to check this, or stretch a piece of string tautly across the board, anchoring it at each end with pins.

Push a pin through each patch to hold it in place when it has been aligned correctly. The second row of patches should then be placed in position—overlapping the first row. The patches should overlap the ends of the hemmed edges of the first row by 6mm ($\frac{1}{4}$in) and also cover the unhemmed edges of the first row

Fig.3

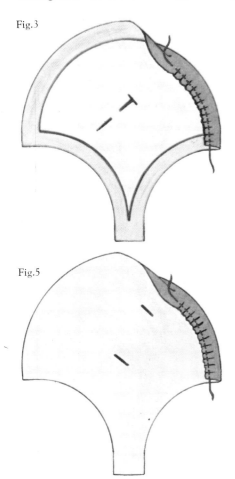

Fig.5

Fig.4

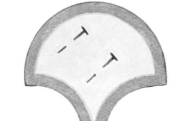

Fig.6

Fig. 3 (Method 1). Basting the hem of the patch to the lining.
Fig. 4 (Method 2). Pinning the card to the right side of the patch.
Fig. 5 Turning the hem to the wrong side and basting.
Fig. 6 The correct positioning of the first two rows of the Fish-scale pattern.

Right, above: A simple top for
a child, made of shell patches with
the colours arranged in straight
rows. Ribbons have been used to
make halter straps and back ties.

Right, below: A tea cosy with the
shell patches arranged in 'V' shapes.

completely. The top centre of each patch in the second row should be in line with the join between patches in the first row.

Pin the second row of patches to the first row and baste the two rows together, following the line of the convex curves.

The final joining of the two rows is worked by hemming neatly around the convex edges of the patches with small slip stitches, on the right side of the work.

If the patches were originally hemmed using card patterns, remove all basting stitches before placing the next row of patches in position. If the patches have been lined, remember that the basting stitches are left in and should not show on the surface of the work. Continue adding one row of patches at a time.

Before the work can be lined, the outside edges must be straightened. A simple way of doing this is to turn under the unwanted half patches on the wrong side. A less wasteful method is to cut off the tops of the patches in the first row and to use them to fill the spaces in the last row.

Chapter 4
Traditional designs

Log Cabin & Pineapple

Log Cabin is unlike any other kind of patchwork. It takes its name from the overlapping logs on the corners of cabins built by early settlers in the States and Canada. It was very popular during the second half of the nineteenth century in America and in England, where it was known as Canadian patchwork. A variation on the same pattern resembled the pineapple, a traditional symbol of hospitality, and so Pineapple quilts were reserved for the guest room.

Originally Log Cabin patchwork must have been developed as one of the simplest and most practical ways of using up scraps of fabric too small and too narrow to be used for anything else.

This kind of patchwork is constructed by the block method. The blocks differ from 'pieced' blocks because all the strips which form the pattern are sewn onto a square of foundation fabric, forming a 'pressed' block. A much wider variety of fabrics can be used in one piece of work than in pieced patchwork, because the foundation fabric bears the strain of heavy wear.

Most old Log Cabin quilts were made from dress and shirt cottons, light wools, worsteds and even from tweeds.

Ribbon patchwork

At one time, Log Cabin patchwork became part of the Victorian fad for multi-coloured 'crazy' patchwork and it was made from richer materials. Satin and velvet ribbons were often used at this time, instead of strips of fabric, and the work became known as Ribbon patchwork. You can copy this idea, using remnants of ribbon which are sometimes sold quite cheaply at haberdashery [notion] counters.

Log Cabin

Log Cabin patchwork is made from strips of light- and dark-coloured fabric sewn onto a foundation around a central square or 'fire'. The finished block is divided either diagonally, or top and bottom, by the light and dark colours. The blocks are always sewn together, or set, edge to edge. They are not separated by plain squares or lattice strips as are some of the pieced or appliqué blocks.

A variety of patterns can be constructed, depending on the way in which the light and dark sections are arranged within the blocks themselves and on the completed piece of work.

In America each arrangement has its own name. For example, if light and dark run diagonally across the work, the pattern is known as Straight Furrows. If the light and dark are grouped on opposite sides of the individual blocks the pattern is called Courthouse Steps.

Innumerable other arrangements are possible, so one way of designing is to make up as many squares of Log Cabin as you need, then move them around until you have an overall pattern of light and dark that you like. But remember that you must decide before you sew on the strips whether you want the light and dark on each separate block to be on opposite or adjacent sides.

Method of working

First decide on the finished size of your patchwork, then divide this into squares. If you are making a large article, like a bedspread, 30cm (12in) blocks are a good average size. For smaller articles, such as cushions or trimmings for clothes, 15cm (6in) squares are more appropriate.

Cut out the required number of foundation squares, allowing 12mm (½in) all round for seams. The foundation squares will be covered completely by the Log Cabin strips, but they will need to take the strain of a variety of fabrics. Calico is a suitable fabric to use.

Decide how wide you want your strips to be. 2.5cm (1in) is a popular size and we use it here as an example. You must also allow 6mm (¼in) on each side for seams.

Templates are not often used in Log Cabin patchwork as you can cut out your strips following the grain of the fabric. However, if you feel happier using one, make a template by drawing a rectangle to the size you require (see page 35); cut out a window from it so that you can see what the patch will look like.

Fabric You will need a square of fabric to form the central square. This is usually twice the width of the strips – so it is 5cm (2in) square in our example – plus a 6mm (¼in) seam allowance all round.

You will need equal amounts of light and dark fabric. It is helpful to draw a pattern on a square of paper, to the same size as your foundation square, so that you can see how long

each strip needs to be. For each square within the block, you will need two dark strips and two light strips. For each journey around the block, they should be 5cm (2in) longer than the previous four strips.

Thus, if you start with a 5cm (2in) central square (plus seam allowance), you will need 10cm (4in) long strips (two light, two dark) for the first square. Then four 15cm (6in) long

Above: Log Cabin blocks have been set together to form the overall pattern known as Barn Raising.

strips (two light and two dark) for the next square, and so on – always adding a 6mm (¼in) seam allowance all round – until you have enough strips to fill the foundation square.

Constructing the block

To place the strips in the correct position, it is helpful if diagonal pencil or basting lines are made on the foundation fabric from corner to corner, crossing in the centre of the square. These lines will act as guides for correct assembly.

Cut out a 5cm (2in) square of fabric for the 'fire'. Place the small square on the foundation block and sew it in place with running stitches (fig.1).

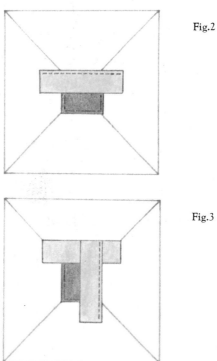

Fig.1

Starting at the top of the 'fire' or central square, place one of the strips right-side down on the foundation square, so that one long edge is against one edge of the central square. Sew it down with running stitches 6mm (¼in) from the edge (fig.2). Fold back the strip and press it down. You can either machine stitch or hand sew the strips down.

The second strip of light fabric is sewn along the second side of the central square, overlapping the first strip at the end (fig.3). Fold back and press. Similarly, the third strip – this

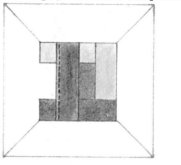

Fig.4

time of dark fabric – is stitched into position, overlapping the second at one end (fig.4). Fold back and press.

The fourth side of the central square is then covered with the fourth strip of dark fabric, this time overlapping both the first and third strips at the ends (fig.5). Fold back and press.

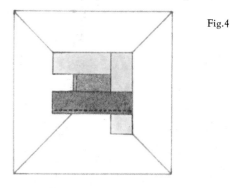

Fig.5

The process is repeated on the next round, starting on the same side, this time covering the edge of the first row of strips.

Continue covering the foundation square in this way, using two strips of light and dark fabric for each square and always starting on the same side of the square. In this way, you will end up with a completely symmetrical pattern, with all the light strips on the opposite diagonal of the completed square (fig.6).

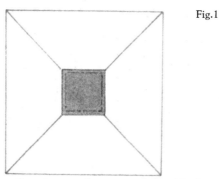

Fig.2

Fig.3

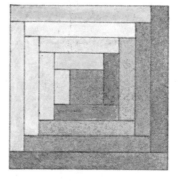

Fig.6

Fig. 1 The centre square basted to the foundation.
Fig. 2 The first strip stitched in position.
Fig. 3 The second strip overlaps the first.
Fig. 4 The third strip overlaps the second strip.
Fig. 5 The fourth strip completes the square.
Fig. 6 The completed Log Cabin block.

Opposite: The photographs show details from three Log Cabin quilts and a Pineapple quilt. Top and bottom left: Two similar methods of setting Log Cabin blocks, which result in different overall effects. Top right: The traditional setting of Log Cabin, known as Straight Furrows. Bottom right: Four blocks from a Pineapple, or Windmill Blades, quilt.

61

Fig. 7 A Courthouse Steps block.
Fig. 8 Constructing the 'V' pattern.
Fig. 9 The completed 'V' pattern.

Below: A Log Cabin bedspread, pillow and matching upholstered panel.

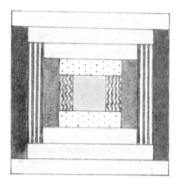

Fig.7

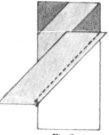

Fig.8

Fig.9

The edges of the final strips should meet with the edges of the foundation square. This will, of course, be hidden when the blocks are eventually joined. To ensure a flat finish when joining the blocks later, baste around the edge of the completed block to hold the final strips and the foundation fabric together.

Although this arrangement of colours is traditional, you could experiment with your own combination of shades if you wish to achieve a different effect.

Log Cabin quilts Because Log Cabin is constructed on a foundation fabric the top layer is very thick and makes quilting almost impossible. If you wish to make a quilt you must line, interline, and tie your finished patchwork by following the instructions on page 27.

Courthouse Steps

Courthouse Steps is a simple variation on the Log Cabin theme (fig.7). The light and dark shades fall on opposite sides of the block. The strips of fabric are built up in a similar way as described for Log Cabin.

The overlap of the strips, however, is slightly different and necessitates the sewing of strips in opposite pairs, rather than working round the block, as for Log Cabin.

'V' pattern

A more unusual design, which appears to have been popular only in Britain, is the 'V' pattern. It is made up by sewing strips of fabric together in

an attractive chevron arrangement.

Light and dark fabrics are stitched together alternately in diagonal strips to narrow lengths of foundation material (fig.8).

The pattern is constructed by joining in the covered lengths so that the strips match in colour on each side of the seam to make a 'V' (fig.9).

Pineapple

Pineapple is a more complicated variation of Log Cabin. It is sometimes known as Windmill Blades (see photograph on previous page).

The Pineapple block is based on the same principle as the Log Cabin, in that strips are sewn on to a foundation block of fabric. The block though is larger – about 45cm (18in) square. It would be difficult to attempt such intricacy within a smaller block.

The strips are sewn in much the same way as for Log Cabin, but in alternate rows of light and dark colours. This design is particularly effective when worked in one plain colour and white.

The positioning of strips is slightly different to that of Log Cabin. On every other journey round the block the strips are laid diagonally across the corners, instead of parallel to the sides of the square.

When complete each square consists of four half 'pineapples' The whole pineapple pattern only emerges when the blocks are joined. The finished block will look as if triangles and trapezoids have been sewn round a diamond.

Mayflower or Cathedral window

This unusual combination of appliqué and patchwork is said to have originated on the Mayflower carrying the Pilgrims from England to America in the seventeenth century. The women on board used old flour sacks as a backing and frame for the tiny precious pieces of coloured fabric. Whether this story is true or not, women in America did use coarse sacking as a foundation fabric. Another descriptive name for this type of patchwork is Cathedral Window.

Mayflower patchwork at first looks as intricate as a Chinese puzzle, but it is in fact extremely simple to make. It is also practical because the foundation fabric forms a neat backing and edging in itself.

The basis of the work is the folding and refolding of squares of the foundation fabric, so the finished work is composed of many layers of fabric and makes a warm light covering without any additional interlining or backing.

Method of working
Nowadays, instead of flour sacks, calico [unbleached muslin] or any light firmly woven fabric makes a good foundation. Plain fabric inset with multi-coloured squares gives a lovely 'cathedral window' effect. You can alternatively use a multi-coloured print as the foundation with 'windows' of plain fabric to pick out the colours in the print.

The method of preparing the found- ation reduces its original size by just over half, so allow 2¼ times the size of the finished article for the foundation fabric.

The squares can be any size; a 15cm (6in) square reduces to 7cm (2¾in). Each square this size needs a patch of contrast fabric 4.5cm (1¾in) square. This will help you to calculate roughly how many squares and 'windows' you will need to make up the finished article.

Mayflower patchwork cannot really be pressed once it is made up, so all the fabrics should be pressed well first.

There are two methods of making up the squares. To understand each method well read all the instructions, following them through with a practice square of fabric.

Making up the squares
Method 1 is suitable for fabrics like calico [unbleached muslin] and cotton that hold a crease well.

Using a square shaped template, or cutting along the grain of the fabric, cut the foundation fabric into 15cm (6in) squares. Fold over and press a turning of 6mm (¼in) all round each square.

Take a square and fold all the corners into the centre. Pin in place (fig.1). The square is now 10cm (4in) long on each side.

Fold each corner into the centre once again, removing each pin and re-

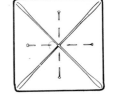

Fig.1

Fig. 1 (Method 1). The corners of a square folded and pinned in the centre.

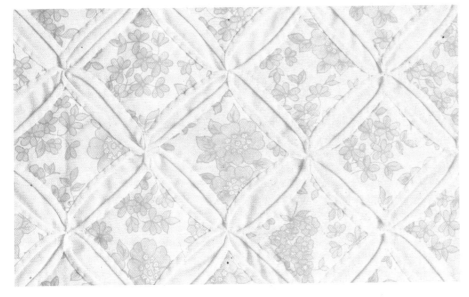

Left: Detail of the Mayflower patchwork cot quilt. A plain fabric has been used for the background, and a toning printed fabric for the centre squares.

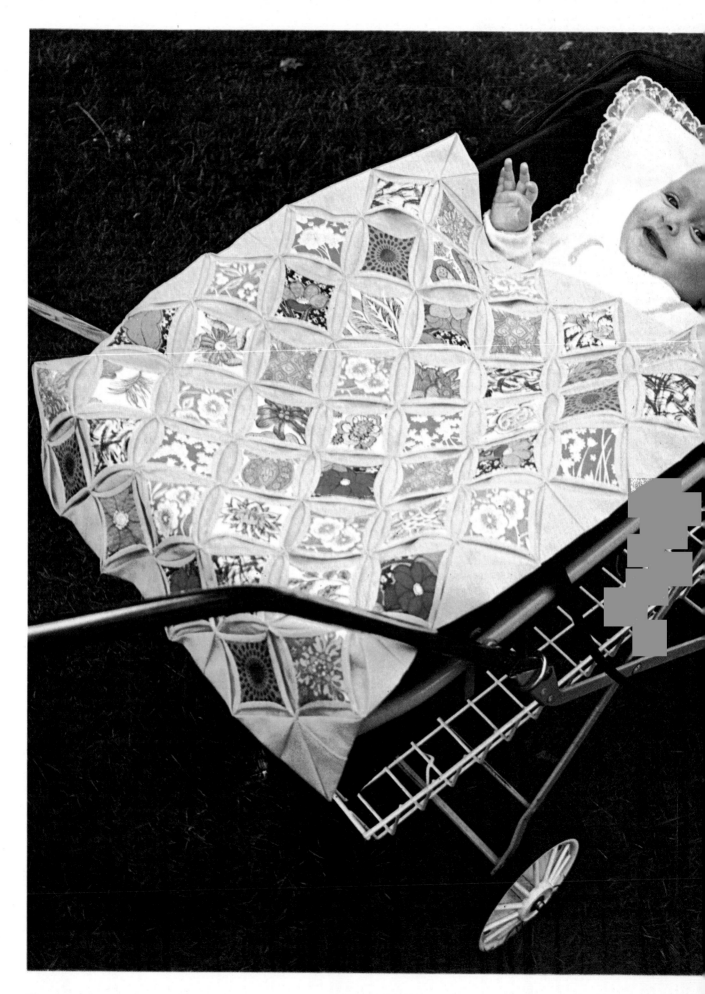

inserting it as you work round the square. The new square will now have sides of approximately 7cm (2¾in).

In the centre of the square, sew the corners in place with two small cross stitches through all the thicknesses of fabric (fig.2).

Make a second square in the same way. Join it to the first, wrong sides together, by oversewing [overcasting] along one edge. Keep the stitches small, especially at the corners.

There is now a diamond shaped 'window' where the two patches are joined. Pin a 4.5cm (1¾in) square of patterned fabric centrally over the join (fig.3). There is no need to make any turnings on the patterned fabric.

The edges are covered as follows. Turn a folded edge of the foundation over one edge of the patterned square so that it lies in a curve. With small even stitches, hem the fold in place neatly, working through all the thicknesses (fig.4). Repeat round all sides of the patterned square, and finally make a small stitch across each corner to keep the turnings neat and firm.

Continue adding foundation patches, attaching window patches to each diamond formed when the foundation squares are joined, and to the extra diamonds formed when the rows of patches are joined.

The triangles along the edges of the work can be left plain, or you can fill them with triangular patches. To do this, turn back the edges of the diamonds in the normal way along two sides. Turn under the third edge of the patch and catch it down.

Method 2 is suitable for fabrics which do not hold a crease well. Sheetings you may want to use often contain synthetic fibres which are too springy to hold a crease without help.

Cut out the foundation squares as before. Fold each square in half and machine or hand sew the shorter edges together, taking a 6mm (¼in) seam allowance (fig.5).

Fold the square again at right angles to the first fold, matching the unstitched edges together.

Stitch one seam diagonally from corner to corner, but on the second seam leave a 2.5cm (1in) opening at the centre for turning (fig.6). Turn the square to the right side and slip stitch the opening.

The square is now 10cm (4in), and is ready for the second folding in of the corners. From this point onwards, proceed in exactly the same way as described in method 1.

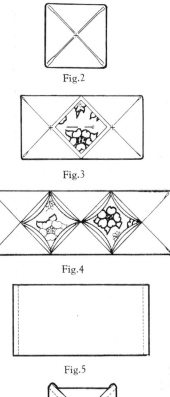

Fig.2

Fig.3

Fig.4

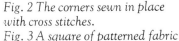

Fig.5

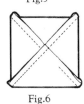

Fig.6

Fig. 2 The corners sewn in place with cross stitches.
Fig. 3 A square of patterned fabric pinned centrally over the join.
Fig. 4 Patterned 'window' patches attached to the diamond which is formed when foundation squares are joined.
Fig. 5 (Method 2). Foundation squares are folded in half and the shorter ends sewn together.
Fig. 6 Two diagonal seams, one with an opening left for turning.

Left: Mayflower patchwork is especially suitable for a pram covering, as it makes a warm fabric without requiring a lining or interlining.

Crazy work & embroidered patchwork

In many ways Crazy patchwork is closer to appliqué than patchwork, as the pieces are stitched to a foundation material rather than to each other. Like Log Cabin, Crazy patchwork was born of necessity, when every tiny scrap that could be salvaged from worn out clothing was valuable.

As the patchwork is stitched to a backing material which takes the strain, many different fabrics can be included in one piece of work. Crazy patchwork, however, is not usually quilted, because of its irregularity.

In the 1880's, Crazy patchwork became extremely popular. 'Only those having seen this fashionable work can imagine its beauty for pillows and quilts . . . very handsome piano covers, antimacassars, sofa pillows and table covers can be arranged', enthused one contemporary observer.

The Victorians, with their love of ornamentation, adored Crazy work, They used the velvets, satins and brocades which were fashionable at the time for clothes and furnishings. Scraps of rich fabric were basted onto a foundation at random and the raw edges covered with lavish embroidery. Not only the edges, but frequently the patches themselves were decorated with embroidery in silk and metallic threads, encrusted with beads, sequins and ribbon work. Sprays of flowers, birds with ribbon work tails, fruit, hearts, stars and figures were all elaborately worked on the patches. The finished work was edged with rich satin frills or scallops.

When the fashion died out and tastes changed, Crazy patchwork was regarded as among the worst examples of Victorian over-ornamentation. Today, Crazy patchwork is regarded more fondly. It is evocative of an opulent age and an ideal way to indulge yourself with the pleasures of lavish stitchery, rich fabrics and glowing jewel-like colours.

If you want to incorporate fabrics with a sentimental value into your patchwork, then this is the perfect way to do it. A quilt made in Louisiana in the late nineteenth century includes Civil War campaign ribbons and army unit badges, as well as carefully embroidered pieces of silk and velvet.

Another is made up of pieces of fabric gathered from a large family. It includes fragments of a lace corset cover, a leather bow tie and a man's hat band. Each piece is embroidered with the donor's dates of birth and death and a line about him or her. The whole quilt must have been completely impractical but it is a wonderful combination of family album and soft art.

Method of working

Collect scraps of all kinds of fabric, the richer and more decorative the better. You can include all sorts of things in this collection, lengths of ribbon, metallic braids and pieces of embroidered fabric. Ties are often made of heavy opulent silks and satins that are ideal for Crazy patchwork.

Press all the scraps and trim off frayed edges and very irregular ends. Sort the collection into piles of light and dark fabrics and then sort them out again into colours.

In theory it seems easy to stitch together a random collection of scraps, but in practice the results can be terrible. Unlike other types of patchwork, which are based on regular geometric shapes that bring an overall unity to the finished article whatever the colours, Crazy patchwork depends almost entirely on colour to be successful. So you should take a lot of time moving the colours around on the foundation fabric until the arrangement satisfies you.

Any strong closely woven cotton will do for the foundation. If you are making a large item, divide it up into blocks. These will make the work easier to handle and the colours easier to plan over a small area. The finished blocks can be joined together with strips of velvet and surrounded by a border. A dark colour used in this way will help to pull all the colours together. The blocks can also be stitched together and the seams covered with embroidery, a couched cord or braid.

Spread the foundation blocks out and plan the arrangement of fabrics and colours on them. Pin each piece of fabric in place as you decide where it will go.

Begin by sewing down a piece of fabric in one corner of the foundation

Opposite: A Crazy work quilt which achieves regularity by intermixing solid squares. Random shapes, outlined in herringbone stitch, have been used for the tea cosy in the foreground.

Below: A detail from the quilt shows the intricate embroidery work.

Above:A nineteenth century quilt of random patches, worked in blocks and embroidered with the maker's signature.

and work outwards from that. Sew each piece down with small running stitches close to the edge. Underlap and overlap the edges as you build up the patchwork. You can turn under the raw edges of each overlapping piece for a stronger neater finish if you wish. The Victorians did not do this because they intended to embroider heavily over all the raw edges.

Decorative stitches and beads

When all the patches have been sewn down, work embroidery stitches over all the edges. Triple feather stitch was a Victorian favourite; it is highly decorative as well as being a practical way of covering the raw edges. A large number of stitches can be used; any feather stitch or herringbone stitch variation, blanket stitch, cross stitch or any

Left: A detail from the quilt shown opposite, illustrating the rich variety of stitching which has been used to decorate the velvet patches and to keep the edges from fraying. Herringbone and feather stitch are popular for this kind of work. They are illustrated, with other useful stitches, on pages 148 and 149.

stitch that will cover the raw edges decoratively. Add as much embroidery to the patches as you wish.

Beads and sequins sewn on at random or in a simple motif on a few patches will add light and a rich texture.

Machined Crazy patchwork

You can make up a piece of patchwork in an afternoon on a sewing machine. If it's a straight stitch machine, simply pin or loosely baste the patches in place and stitch them down. Then work embroidery over the edges by hand.

If you have a swing needle machine, work a wide zigzag stitch over all the edges. Then either embroider by hand or work machine satin stitch over the edges to finish off. If your machine also does a variety of embroidery stitches, then you can simply sew the patches straight down with a decorative stitch.

Embroidery and patchwork

Embroidery and patchwork are not often combined in traditional work except in Crazy patchwork, although small motifs were also sometimes embroidered on the central square of a Log Cabin block.

Patches themselves, however, can be cut from partly worn embroideries. These patches add extra colour and texture to patchwork. They are also a good way of using pretty embroidery that has been worked on no-longer fashionable clothes or furnishings.

If you would like to combine embroidery with your patchwork, then work the embroidery within the outlines of the patches before cutting them out. Alternatively, embroidery can be worked when the patchwork is complete. If you want the embroidery to be a feature of the patchwork without creating a lavish 'crazy' effect, then keep the patchwork shapes and patterns fairly simple. Use plain rather than print fabrics and limit the range of colours.

Decorative stitches were often used by the Victorians to embroider signatures on a piece of patchwork. This technique can be used today to add a personal touch to a quilt.

Suffolk puffs

Suffolk Puffs are also known as Yorkshire Daisy and Puffball in England and Yo Yo in America. This is a purely decorative form of patchwork as the puffs do not join up into a solid fabric. The patchwork can be lined with a plain fabric that will show through the spaces between the puffs.

A simple multi-coloured arrangement of Suffolk Puffs looks very attractive as a decorative bedspread. Puffs can also be sewn together in a triangular shape to make a light shawl.

Suffolk Puffs can be threaded through the middle on strong linen thread to make simple floppy toys for babies. A snake can be as long as you like. Make the head from a circle of fabric filled with wadding [batting]. Run a row of stitches around the edge, decorate the head with embroidery or appliqué and thread on a long body. A rag doll or clown can be made in the same way with large puffs for the body and smaller ones for the arms and legs. Bright colours are ideal for these toys.

Method of working

Each puff is made from a circle of fabric, saucer sized, about 12.5cm (5in) in diameter. Light cotton that will gather easily is the best fabric.

Turn the edge of the fabric down on the wrong side about 6mm ($\frac{1}{4}$in) and using double thread, work a row of running stitches all round the circle.

Pull up the gathers tightly, knot the thread and press the circle flat. Join the edges of the circles where they touch with three flat satin stitches.

Opposite: A simple arrangement of colours in a Suffolk Puffs quilt.

Below: A more complex arrangement of colours in a silk bedspread.

Fig. 1 Running stitches worked all around the circle.
Fig. 2 The gathers pulled up and the thread knotted.

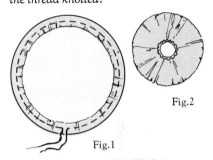

Fig.1   Fig.2

Other traditional designs

In many ways the borderline between appliqué and patchwork is indistinct. There are a number of patterns that are constructed by a combination of these two needle arts, although they are usually considered as part of the patchwork tradition.

Some of these patterns are made up of regular geometric patchwork shapes. The Star of Bethlehem is one example. It is composed of a patchwork of diamonds and when complete is appliquéd to a background fabric. Rosettes of hexagons are another example as they are often appliquéd, particularly as a border pattern.

Other patterns are made up of shapes that are unique to that particular pattern. You will probably have to make your own templates for all patterns of this type.

Grandmother's Fan

Grandmother's Fan is an attractive design that looks most effective made from a variety of prints with a plain dark centre on a light-coloured background.

To make the pattern Draw a 30.5cm (12in) square for the basic block. Then, draw two arcs across the block and divide the fan into six equal leaves. This is done by measuring six angles of 15° from the corner of the block, using a protractor. When cutting out the fabric, add 6mm ($\frac{1}{4}$in) all round for turnings.

You can baste all the patches over papers and sew them together like regular patchwork, but the quickest and most common technique is to use the 'pressed' method. This means that the leaves of the fan are sewn directly onto the foundation square in the same way as the Log Cabin pattern is put together.

Method of working

Cut out a 30.5cm (12in) square of foundation fabric, adding a seam allowance. Baste down the first leaf of the fan at the top of the block leaving the edges raw. Place the second leaf face down on top of the first, matching the lower edges.

Sew them together through all the layers of fabric, 6mm ($\frac{1}{4}$in) from the edge. Fold the second leaf down, right

side up, and press the seam. Add the other four leaves in the same way.

Turn under the curved edge of the small central semi-circle and stitch it down, covering the raw edges of the fan. The outer raw edges can be turned under and stitched down, or they can be covered with bias strips in the same colour as the semi-circle. The sewing can be done by hand or machine.

Like Log Cabin patchwork, the blocks can be arranged in various ways to create an overall pattern. They can be sewn together flush with the fans all spreading their arcs in the same direction, or with the fans spreading in alternate directions.

One popular way of making up a Grandmother's Fan quilt was to set the blocks in groups of four, separated by narrow strips of plain fabric with the fans in each group facing inwards.

Dresden Plate

The Dresden Plate pattern, in which the leaves form a complete circle, is made in the same way as Grandmother's Fan, but cutting and sewing have to be accurate to bring the leaves

Below and bottom: The Prairie Flower and Tulip designs.

Right: Grandmother's Fan – the fan is pieced together and sewn to the foundation.

Opposite: A detail of the child's cot quilt, shown on page 75. The block shown here is an adaptation of the Dresden Plate design. Hexagons, instead of the traditional circle, cover the centre of the leaves.

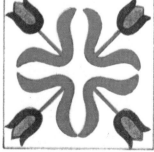

Above: The Flower Basket design.
The basket is pieced and the flowers
appliquéd to the foundation block.

Top: The Cock's Comb design.

Right: A traditional Dresden Plate
quilt which has been designed so
that no two blocks are identical in
colour and print combinations. The
story of its origins has been
embroidered on it.

round to meet evenly.

To make the pattern The pattern can
be made to any size, depending on
whether you want to use it as a large
central motif or smaller on single
blocks. To draw your own pattern,
draw a large circle, then a slightly
smaller circle just inside. The points of
the leaves will touch the outer circle.

To make a plate with 18 leaves,
draw a line from the centre out to the
edge of the smaller circle. Measure an
angle of 10° using a protractor and
extend this angle to the edge of the
outer circle. Repeat the measurement,
extending the angle to the edge of the
inner circle. Join up the three points on
the edges of the circles to make one
leaf.

You need only draw one leaf, the
rest are exactly the same. Draw in the
small central circle. Add 6mm (¼in) all

round for seams when cutting out the fabric.

The leaves of the Dresden Plate can be used in other ways besides stitching them into the traditional full circle. They can be sewn in an arc radiating from the corner of a square, to create a sunray effect. Alternatively, you can arrange ten leaves into a butterfly shape and appliqué an oval-shaped 'body' over the inner raw edges.

Star patterns

Complicated many-pointed star patterns are also made by methods which combine appliqué with patchwork.

The Sun Burst pattern is made up of

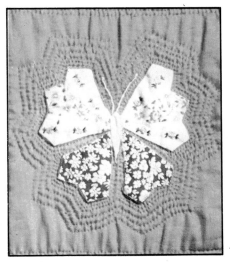

Left, above: A child's cot quilt and a detail from it. The quilt is an unusual combination of appliquéd hearts, hexagonal rosettes and Dresden Plate 'leaves'. Quilting stitches follow the outline of the applied patchwork. The detail is an adaptation of the Dresden Plate design. Ten 'leaves' are arranged in a butterfly shape, with an oval-shaped 'body' applied over the raw edges.

Left, below: A Rose of Sharon block, also known as Ohio Rose and California Rose. It has been made up in the traditional colours of this design.

Below and bottom: The Noon Day Lily and Maple Leaf designs, both combining piecing and appliqué.

a number of elongated pyramid triangles. The triangles are sewn to the background fabric in three layers. The bottom layer, usually in a light colour, is made up of 16 triangles appliquéd to the background fabric in a full circle. Eight triangles in a darker colour are then sewn between every second point of the first circle A third circle is made of eight more triangles in a contrasting fabric Finally, a circle is sewn down in the centre to cover the raw edges.

An adapted diamond 'kite' shape is used to build up a star in the same way In this pattern, however, each diamond is made up of two contrasting fabrics.

Hearts

Hearts are a popular motif which were traditionally appliquéd to marriage quilts and quilts made for babies and young children The Hearts and Kisses pattern, often seen on Marriage quilts, was made up of four hearts with their points facing inwards, the 'kisses' were implied in the X-shaped space between the hearts.

Although this is a traditional appliqué motif, four hearts can also be treated as patchwork shapes and stitched together to make a round-pointed star.

A further variation is to cut each heart in half and make up the star in two different fabrics. The fabric should be basted over papers and the patches sewn together like regular patchwork. The finished star should then be appliquéd to a background fabric.

Right: This delightful quilt, with its striking colour scheme, is a show piece of combination blocks. It includes two traditional designs – Little Beech Tree (bottom left) and Peony (middle right).

Left: Adapted diamond 'kite' shapes, in two contrasting fabrics, forming a Sun Burst pattern.

Below: Three patchwork pictures. The Basket and the Tulip are two traditional designs, in contrast with the third pattern which is a modern adaptation of Log Cabin.

Chapter 5
Introduction to appliqué

The history of appliqué

Appliqué is one of the simplest and certainly one of the oldest ways of decorating cloth. It has a universal appeal, as it is not only part of the needlework tradition of many nations, but also one of the most popular forms of needlework today.

In a busy modern world where many traditional forms of needlework are considered too time consuming for any but a handful of enthusiasts, large appliqué designs can be put together in no time with the help of a sewing machine. The pleasure and excitement of creating individual designs has been enhanced by the enormous range of fabrics, colours and textures that are easily available to everyone.

The name appliqué derives from the Latin *applicare*, to fold or to fasten to, and it is probably a good deal older than patchwork. Like patchwork, it developed from the very basic necessity for repair. The simplest way to strengthen a worn place or repair a hole is to cover it with a patch cut from another fabric. If the worn fabric is part of clothing, then pride in appearance would naturally lead to making the patch appear as something decorative.

Not only is appliqué an obvious method of making repairs, it is one of the quickest ways of making decorative designs, as comparatively large areas of a design can be created in one operation.

Appliqué world-wide

People all over the world have worked appliqué using the local materials that were available to them. Thousands of years ago, Indians in Arizona stitched dried leaves to leather. Farther north, Canadian Indians living in the Artic decorated their caribou skin garments with designs cut from the soft skin of the underbelly. They inlaid them into the tough hide that made up the main part of the garment. On the other side of the world, the Maoris of New Zealand stitched brightly coloured feathers to bark. Traditional Japanese appliqué is heavily padded and includes gold and silver leaf as well as silk.

Appliqué is often regarded as a purely masculine skill. In Tibet, men made rich intricate temple hangings in silk and decorated their tents, clothes and saddle blankets with appliqué designs in felt. The Fon of Dahomey on the west coast of Africa associate appliqué with civil and military power and it is worked only by men. Traditionally, an exclusive family guild of artists lived in a compound close to their king making symbolic heraldic hangings, banners, umbrellas and ritual clothing. Tribal history, ritual and mythology were depicted in motifs cut from brilliantly coloured cotton. Appliqué is still part of the artistic tradition, although now the customers are not kings but tourists.

The Cuna Indian women of the San Blas islands off the coast of Panama have developed one of the most unusual forms of appliqué, appliqué in reverse. Instead of laying pieces of cloth on a background, designs are created by cutting away layers of cloth to reveal the brilliant colours of the layers underneath. Their designs too are taken from tribal mythology. They also include motifs taken from the life around them. Natural objects, animals and flowers, are combined with symbols of the modern world – people and events seen on television and designs taken from advertisements.

Historical examples

In Europe, appliqué was highly developed by the Middle Ages. Old manuscripts show that it was commonly used for making banners and heraldic devices. It was also an important part of the great medieval English tradition of ecclesiastical embroidery. Motifs cut from rich silks and damasks were applied to vestments and altar cloths and decorated with embroidery in silk and gold threads.

Many historical examples survive in churches, museums and the great country houses of England. Among the most splendid surviving examples of appliqué are a set of panelled hangings in Hardwick Hall in Derbyshire. The work was done by the Countess of Shrewsbury, Bess of Hardwick. Some of the rich materials used in the appliqué hangings are believed to have been taken, and cut up from,

Facing previous page: Simple, bold tulip motifs have been applied to a co-ordinating cot liner and bed cover.

Opposite: The centre panel from the Marion Hanging, which was made by Bess, Countess of Shrewsbury c. 1570 at Hardwick Hall. She was helped by Mary Queen of Scots during the latter's imprisonment there. The Queen's initials (MR) can be seen on the lower panel. The centre panel bears the Royal Arms of Scotland and the lower panel the monograms of the Earl and Countess of Shrewsbury. The Hanging is an excellent example of early English appliqué. The centre panel is made of fine canvas, embroidered with silk in tent stitch, and appliquéd to a background of green velvet.

VULNERE

VIRESCIT VIRTVS

GEORGE E L

Above: A detail from a nineteenth century American quilt. The design is known as Ohio Farmyard and shows how the lives of patchworkers were reflected in their quilts. Traditionally, in America, quilt tops were divided into a number of repeating blocks, with appliquéd patterns. The importance given to the names of these designs is a characteristic of American quiltmaking.

beautiful old church vestments.

Mary Queen of Scots, while a prisoner at Hardwick Hall, worked several appliqué hangings and long cushions. Much of the Queen's work included needlepoint motifs appliquéd to a velvet background. It is possible that she brought this technique with her from France.

In those days, when ladies spent many hours embroidering needlepoint canvas for cushions and hangings, appliqué was something of an innovation and became very fashionable. By working only the needlepoint motifs and applying them to another fabric, many tedious hours spent embroidering the canvas background were avoided. Stylized flowers and shrubs were the most common motifs. They were worked first in petit point in silk, then applied to a silk or velvet background and edged and connected with gold thread.

The value of appliqué as an economical way of using old fabrics was realised by the rich as well as the poor. Bess of Hardwick was not the only thrifty lady to take rich embroidery and apply it to make something entirely different. A set of curtains at Corsham Court in Wiltshire are decorated with appliqué of embroidered cream and crimson satin and velvet. These fabrics were originally part of the mule trappings and coverings of the state coach made by the ladies of Lisbon for Mr John Methuen while he was in Portugal at the end of the seventeenth century.

The eighteenth century

Appliqué is the ideal way to preserve the most precious parts of a precious fabric by cutting them out and applying them to a newer or cheaper background fabric. Printed Indian chintz was all the rage at the beginning of the eighteenth century in England and America. However, to protect British textile manufacturers, the importation of these printed and painted calicoes was forbidden by Act of Parliament in 1701. This only made chintz more desirable than ever. It was the height of fashion and greatly sought after for furnishing and dressmaking.

There was never enough chintz to make a whole bedspread, so women carefully cut out every single motif, re-arranged them and applied them to cheaper white or unbleached calico. They called this technique Persian Embroidery, or Broderie Perse. The shapes of the motifs were accented with blanket stitching or softened with feather stitching.

British manufacturers soon caught onto this fashion and began making special printed patterns for appliqué. Game birds, like pheasants and partridges were the most popular motifs.

Appliqué with patchwork and embroidery

In both England and America, appliqué and patchwork are tradition-

ally combined, especially in quilt making. In England, medallion quilts of the eighteenth and nineteenth centuries often had an elaborately worked appliqué design in the centre, framed by a series of patchwork borders. An appliqué border often finished off a patchwork quilt.

In America, where a quilt top is frequently divided into a number of repeating pattern squares or 'blocks', there are as many appliqué patterns as there are patchwork patterns, each with its own name.

Quite often, motifs were pieced together from geometric patchwork shapes and then applied to a background. Stars made of diamond patches and rosettes of hexagons were often used in this way. There are a number of all-over patterns like Flower Basket or Meadow Lily where the main motif is of pieced patchwork. This is then applied with other curving appliqué shapes added. The Flower Basket, made of triangle patches, has a curved handle and appliqué flowers added, while the Meadow Lily is given a curving stem and leaves.

Many patterns that are commonly categorised as patchwork, Log Cabin, Crazy work, Grandmother's Fan and Dresden Plate for example, owe more to appliqué techniques than to patchwork.

Appliqué is combined with embroidery even more often than with patchwork. The rich appliqué worked on church vestments in ancient times

and today, is further enriched with embroidery in gold and silk. Precious embroideries are frequently re-cycled by being used as appliqué motifs. Appliqué is such a bold form of decoration that some embroidery is usually necessary to add details to the motifs.

Appliqué today

Today, appliqué is an extremely popular form of needlework. It is so versatile; there are so many traditional styles to choose from – San Blas, Shadow appliqué, appliqué Perse – each of which creates a totally different effect from any other. There are endless ways of experimenting, using new materials with old techniques, modern machine techniques with modern styles. To take one of the simplest examples, imagine just how different San Blas appliqué would look if you used different colours, say black, grey, white and blue, instead of the traditional bright colour scheme.

Padding and stuffing can turn appliqué into soft sculpture; plastic-coated fabrics and new synthetic materials add new textures; a sewing machine makes whole new techniques available and takes weeks of tedious sewing time off a project so that the only hand sewing can be creative and enjoyable embroidery.

Today, appliqué is basically a bold technique, a very experimental technique and a needlework art of exciting possibilities.

Above: Garden Wreath, another nineteenth century American design. The floral shapes could be padded or stuffed as they are applied, either to replace or complement the more traditional quilting.

Designing appliqué

Potential appliqué designs are everywhere. Even if you do not feel confident of your ability to draw, there are plenty of ways in which you can work out unique designs and pictures.

Some people like to work directly with cloth, cutting out shapes freehand or following a rough chalk outline. You could start with a simple design in mind and see what effects can be achieved by using scissors as drawing and cutting instruments at the same time.

Alternatively, you could just cut out a random selection of fabric shapes and group and re-group them on a background fabric to form a design.

Working directly with fabric in this way can be very stimulating to the imagination and gives your work a spontaneous liveliness. Experimenting can be very enjoyable and you may be surprised when you see the results you have produced.

Working out designs

Most of the time you will probably want to work out a design first, however roughly, on paper. Try working out designs by folding and cutting squares of paper in the same way that children make snow flakes.

You could try making a design from an exploded shape. To do this, cut out a large bold shape, a square or a circle, for example. Draw a series of curved or straight lines on the shape. Then cut along these lines and re-arrange the 'exploded' pieces into a design, moving them around until a satisfactory pattern emerges. Be aware of the pattern formed by the spaces of exposed background fabric as well as the superimposed patterns.

Also consider adding embroidery or other decorations to the design. For

Right: The textures as well as the patterns of the fabric used for this cushion have been carefully chosen.

Far right: An exotic wall hanging which is an excellent example of appliqué design at its best.
The fabrics and colours harmonize beautifully with the animal and floral motifs.

example, certain shapes could be boldly outlined as they are applied, or highlighted later with embroidery. Lines of couching or embroidery could form a pattern on top of the shapes, linking separate parts of the appliqué into the whole design.

Another way to arrange shapes into a design is to cut out a number of different shapes, circles, stars, triangles, or use gummed paper shapes. Use abstract designs from tiles, paintings or textiles, or look through books for examples of particular styles like Art Deco or oriental art.

Design ideas
Keep a folder of designs or pictures that appeal to you. Magazine and newspaper photographs or advertisements and postcards are good sources for designs. Children's book illustrations are full of adaptable possibilities, from fairy-tale animals to supermen.

You need not copy a complete picture. You can trace off the parts of a picture that you want to use, then enlarge or reduce the scale to the size you need and combine them with parts of a different picture.

Birds or animals, cars or trains, clowns, cartoons, even dinosaurs, can all be adapted in this way as long as the basic shapes are sufficiently simple to be easily cut out and applied. Remember to keep appliqué shapes simple in outline and fairly large. Intricate details are much easier to add later with a few simple embroidery stitches. Unless you are working to a large scale, fiddly details like eyes and claws, veins on leaves, twigs, stalks and details on flowers are more easily and effectively worked in embroidery.

Preparing designs

Enlarging and reducing Use this simple method to enlarge or reduce designs to any size you want. Take a tracing of the design (fig.1) and stick it over a piece of graph paper. Draw a rectangle to enclose the design and number the squares (fig.2). Then draw (preferably on tracing paper, as before) a second rectangle to the size that you want the finished design to be and in the same proportions as the first one. Do this by tracing two adjacent sides of the first rectangle and the diagonal from where they meet. Extend these and draw in the other sides of the second rectangle (fig.3). Divide this into the same number of squares as the smaller one. Finally, carefully copy the design square by square (fig.4).

The final design

Make a full scale drawing of your final design on paper. Mark in the various sections which are to be cut from different fabrics and note where sections are to overlap. Ears, wings or paws, for instance, can be cut out separately and positioned with one edge under the main part of the motif. This makes sewing easier by avoiding difficult angles.

Trace the outline of each section separately onto another piece of paper and cut them out to use as patterns. If you are working with woven fabrics, you should match the straight grain of the appliqué to the straight grain of the background fabric, otherwise the appliqué is likely to pucker and will not lie flat. You should be especially careful to match the grains if the appliqué is to be worked on clothes or

Below: Figs. 1 to 4 show how to enlarge a design to the size you require.

Fig. 1 Draw the design onto tracing paper

Fig. 2 Lay the tracing paper over the graph paper; draw a rectangle to enclose the design, and number the squares in it.

Fig. 3 Draw the second rectangle by tracing two sides and a diagonal from the first and extend as required.

Fig. 4 Transfer the design, square by square, until it is complete.

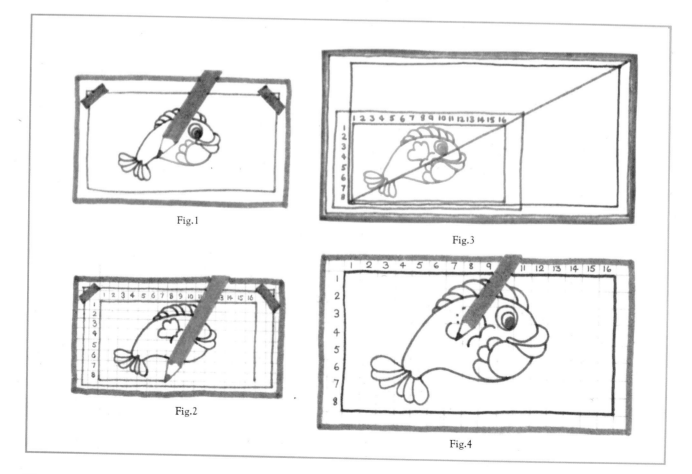

Fig.1

Fig.2

Fig.3

Fig.4

anything that will be subject to hard wear. If you do not, the appliqué is likely not only to pucker, but to split if it is subject to strain. Small curved motifs can be cut on the cross [bias]. Refer to your original drawing of the design and mark the straight grain on each pattern piece.

You will need to mark some indication of the position of the appliqué on the background fabric. If the design is to be placed centrally on a square, fold the background fabric and the design vertically and horizontally to find the centres and match them up. Alternatively, outline the whole design lightly in pencil or chalk. You can trace it onto the background fabric using an embroidery transfer pencil or dressmaker's carbon paper.

Another method is to draw the design on tissue paper, pin this to the background fabric, baste around the design lines, then tear the paper away.

Below: The success of this design stems from the delicate use of patterned fabrics. The blue and white spots of the strawberries are echoed by the stronger blue spots in the flower on the turtle's back; and again in the unifying border of the cushion, which acts as a frame. The use of a quilted background fabric and the embroidered features on the turtle give subtle variations in texture.

Basic tools & suitable fabrics

One of the advantages of appliqué is that in its simplest form it can be tackled by any beginner, whether by hand or on a machine. If you are new to this needle art you can start with the easiest stitches while you learn the basic skills. Then you can progress to more difficult stitches, which will in turn stimulate you to try out the different techniques which are explained in the next chapter. Before starting a practice sampler, or embarking on a project, you should collect together all the tools and fabrics that you will need so that your work can progress without any interruptions.

Basic tools

Even the most complicated and intricate appliqué can be worked with the simplest tools. Basically, all you need are scissors, pins and a needle and thread.

To plan your own designs you will also need some drawing materials. These should include drawing and tracing paper, a soft pencil and tailor's chalk or dressmaker's carbon paper for transferring designs to fabric.

Work out your design then draw it to its finished size. You can use sheets of wrapping paper or newspaper, taped together if necessary, for really large pieces. Cut out each appliqué motif in paper and use the paper shapes as templates.

Scissors and pins

Two pairs of scissors are useful for cutting out fabric. One large pair of dressmaking scissors and one small pair with very sharp, fine points for cutting small shapes accurately. You will also need a separate pair for cutting paper as this blunts the blades, making them unsuitable for cutting fabric neatly.

Ordinary dressmaking pins are suitable for appliqué. Do not put pins in around the edges of a motif, but put them with their points facing in to the centre of the motif. This helps the appliqué to lie flat on the background fabric and prevents puckering.

Thread

A varied collection of threads gives greater scope for the decoration of your appliqué. For straightforward hand or machine sewing you will need sewing thread to match the colour of the appliqué fabric.

You will also need basting thread in a different colour from the appliqué and the background. If stitchery is to be a feature of your appliqué, whether for sewing down shapes or for adding embroidery, you will need a wide variety of threads. Try and collect as many as you can in a range of colours; they will be as stimulating to design as a good collection of fabrics.

Embroidery threads come in all thicknesses and can be shiny or matt, tightly twisted or stranded. Wool threads can be stitched or couched down. You can use crewel and tapestry wools, rug wool or left-over lengths of knitting and crochet yarn. Glitter threads sold for knitting, gold and silver embroidery threads, raffia, string, ribbon, cord and braid can all be used.

Once you become interested in appliqué, particularly if you enjoy picture making, you will want to start collecting all sorts of other things that can be included in appliqué – beads, sequins, pieces of metal and even stones or shells.

Needles

Crewel needles with sharp points and long eyes are the most versatile, followed by sharps. As you start to include a wider variety of threads and fabrics in your appliqué, you will find other types of needles useful: chenille needles with sharp points and very large eyes for the bulkiest threads; long fine beading needles so that you can attach tiny beads; and glovers' needles, with triangular points that will not split leather or suede, which can be bought for hand or machine sewing.

Sewing machine

A sewing machine really speeds up appliqué. You can apply motifs with an ordinary machine using straight stitch, but the swing needle model is more versatile. Zigzag stitch is useful for covering raw edges and a close zigzag, or satin stitch, makes a firm and decorative edging in one operation.

Opposite: One of the appliqué panels from the zodiac quilt shown on pages 124 and 125. This Virgo panel illustrates how different fabrics can be successfully combined: velvet has been used for the grass and hills; satin for the sky, moon, stars, dress and features. Embroidery stitches have been used to emphasize the outline of the motifs and for the sickle and flowers.

You may find it worthwhile to buy machine embroidery thread if you do a lot of machine appliqué. It comes in large reels and is finer than ordinary dressmaking thread so that if you are working a solid stitch, for instance close zigzag or satin stitch, the stitching will be less obtrusive.

Frame

It is advisable always to work appliqué in a frame. For a really smooth finish with no puckering, the background fabric should be stretched flat, but not pulled too taut because the appliqué fabric should be at the same tension. If the fabrics are at different tensions it will eventually cause puckering and spoil the look of the work.

The advantage of a frame is that it makes it much easier to use certain techniques like couching and padding. It also gives a firm flat surface on which to work.

With some machine and fashion appliqué it will not always be possible to use a frame if the piece of work is very large. In these cases, the background fabric should be laid flat on a table or on the floor. Pinning and basting should be done carefully and thoroughly, keeping all the layers of fabric flat.

For very small items you can use a circular embroidery frame, but make sure that the top hoop does not get pushed over the appliqué as this can crush the work out of shape.

A rectangular slate frame, or even an old picture frame, is best for appliqué. Rectangular frames will only take fabric as wide as they are themselves, but excess length can be wound around the rollers at the top and bottom.

Suitable fabrics

Almost any material can be applied to another. Various people throughout the world have worked appliqué using fish skins, bark, feathers, gold and silver leaf. Today, people who enjoy creative appliqué have a vast range of materials at their disposal. Not only cloth, but also leather, metal and all kinds of objects that have been found or collected make appliqué a lively modern art form.

A wide variety of fabrics is as stimulating to appliqué design as it is to patchwork. Try to make your fabrics work for you. You will soon find that you are looking at fabric with new eyes. Cut motif shapes out in tracing paper and use them like the window template in patchwork, moving each one over the fabric until the details in the pattern are in the best position for cutting out. A spot can become the eye of a bird or animal, or a line of stylized daisies could be placed so that they march down the back of a cat.

Look at prints to see how they harmonise with parts of a design. Large prints will often have animals, flowers or leaves that can be cut out directly from the fabric. A piece of fabric with a tiny flower print can become a whole flower garden or can be cut into the shape of single large flowers. Small prints will be in scale if they are to be used as clothes for figures in a design. A large leafy print can be cut into individual leaves, a tree or a whole forest. Look at different patterns to see how they can be used to your advantage, to enhance all the parts of a design.

Texture

Choose fabrics for texture as well as pattern. A knubbly tweed can be an animal, a wall or a hillside, brown corduroy can be ploughed fields or tree trunks, glitter fabrics can be used for metal or water. Net and nylon stockings can be crumpled up and stitched down or they can be laid over other fabrics to soften areas of colour.

The texture of leather and suede adds something extra to appliqué pictures – a piece of suede could be used for a tree trunk for example. The same applies to clothes – a simple leather motif can turn an ordinary jacket into something much more exclusive and expensive-looking. Lace, knitting and crochet cut from old clothes can also add lively texture.

The choice of fabrics for each project depends on whether or not the finished article is intended for hard wear and laundering. If you are decorating casual or children's clothes you will have to choose appliqué fabrics that can stand up to the same heavy treatment as the background fabric. The appliqué fabric should have a firm, close weave that will not pucker, stretch out of shape or fray too easily. Generally, it should be equal or lighter in weight than the background fabric. Cotton or cotton and synthetic mixtures, depending on the background fabric, are the best fabrics to use for any appliqué that is intended to take a lot of hard wear.

The background fabric

If you want to apply a fabric that is

Left: A design called 'Asparagus', which has successfully combined chiffon with silk and velvet. Embroidery stitches, including long and short stitch, French knots and chain stitch provide additional texture.

heavier than the background fabric, then you can strengthen the latter with strong cotton or calico [unbleached muslin]. Cut a piece the same size as the background fabric, or larger all round than the appliqué design, depending on how much of the background will be covered by the appliqué. Match the grain of the background to the grain of the strengthening material and baste the strengthening material to the wrong side of the background. It is important that the grains match, otherwise unsightly bulges and puckering are likely to appear on the wrong side of the work and the finished appliqué will not lie flat.

Work the appliqué treating the strengthened background as one fabric. When the appliqué is complete, you can either make up the article leaving the strengthening material in place, or trim away the excess fabric on the back of the work.

Interfacing

Interfacing is a useful aid to successful appliqué. It adds extra strength to appliqué fabrics that are flimsy or likely to fray easily. Iron-on interfacing is especially useful as once it is bonded to the appliqué fabric the two can be treated as one fabric.

Iron-on interfacing can be cut out to the exact size of the appliqué shape, then bonded to the appliqué fabric.

Using the interfacing as a guide, cut out the shape adding 6mm ($\frac{1}{4}$in) all round. Turn under the raw edges as you stitch the appliqué down.

Non-fraying fabrics

Non-fraying fabrics are the easiest to use for appliqué. Felt will not stand washing but it is ideal for picture making or for purely decorative articles. Suede and leather should be washable or able to be dry cleaned if they are to be applied to clothes. You may have to mount the background fabric before applying any but the softest leathers. Before you begin applying suede or leather, check to see if they will be permanently marked by pins. If so, secure them to the fabric with a spot of glue. You should use a glover's needle with a triangular point to sew them down.

Plastic-coated materials are tough, practical and washable but they can, however, be marked by pins and basting stitches so you should pin over the edges of shapes or secure with glue or adhesive [cellophane] tape. Use a glover's needle and button thread for sewing. If you are sewing by hand, bring the needle straight up and down rather than slanting it through the plastic. If you are sewing by machine, the plastic may stick under the presser foot – if this happens sprinkle it with a little talcum or French chalk.

Below: A number of different leathers and suedes have been used for the appliqué shapes on the flap of this handbag.

Chapter 6
Appliqué techniques

Handsewn appliqué

There are a number of different ways of working appliqué by hand and some of the techniques are especially suited to particular fabrics. Some methods are intended to be unobtrusive and almost invisible, so that nothing interferes with the contrast between the background and the appliqué. Other methods are more obvious and the attaching stitches must be considered as part of the whole design. If the stitching is worked in a colour matching the appliqué it tends to make the outline softer; in a contrasting colour it makes a bold outline around shapes.

The method you choose depends partly on the fabric you are using and partly on the effect you want to achieve. Some methods require an extra allowance for turning under raw edges on the appliqué. With others, no turnings are needed. Read through the various methods before you cut out any appliqué shapes.

Basting

There are two methods: you can either baste around the edge of the motif, or take the basting stitches right across the centre of each shape. The second method helps to keep the motif lying completely flat.

Non-fraying fabrics

To apply fabrics which do not fray, place the paper template on the wrong side of the fabric and draw round it with pencil or chalk. Cut out each appliqué motif and pin and baste it into place on the background fabric.

Stab stitch is the most unobtrusive way of applying motifs in felt, leather or plastic-coated materials. There are two methods of working. For both use a thread that matches the colour of the appliqué.

Method 1 Bring the needle up through the background fabric and motif, close to the edge of the motif. Then, making a very small stitch, take the needle down again through the two thicknesses (fig.1).

Method 2 Bring the needle up from the background fabric immediately outside the edge of the motif, then take it down again a fraction inside the edge (fig.2).

Non-fraying fabrics can also be applied using any decorative stitch.

Applying non-fraying woven fabrics

You can cut out motifs in most firmly woven fabrics and apply them successfully without turning under the edges. Oversew [overcast] the motif close to the edge first (fig. 3), then baste it on the background fabric and stitch it into place with closely worked blanket stitch, covering the oversewing completely (fig.4).

Bonding

For quick results appliqué shapes can be bonded to the background. The bonding material consists of a non-woven adhesive web which has a special paper backing [fusible fleece].

Cut a piece of bonding slightly larger than the motif, draw the outline of the shape on the paper backing and iron on to the wrong side of the appliqué material (fig.5a). Allow the adhesive to cool and cut out the motif shape. The non-woven adhesive web is now fused to the back of the motif.

Peel off the paper (fig.5b), place the motif, right side up, on the background

Opposite: A wall hanging which combines hand and machine appliqué. Russian braid has been hand sewn around some of the leaf motifs, and chain stitch has been used to emphasize others.

Figs. 1-5 Applying non-fraying fabrics.
Fig. 1 Stab stitch, Method 1.
Fig. 2 Stab stitch, Method 2.
Fig. 3 Oversewing [overcasting] the edges of a motif before applying with blanket stitch.
Fig. 4 Blanket (simple buttonhole) stitch.
Figs. 5a Bonding [fusible fleece] ironed onto the motif fabric.
Fig. 5b Peeling the backing from the motif.

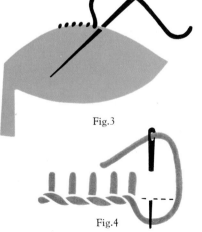

Fig.3

Fig.4

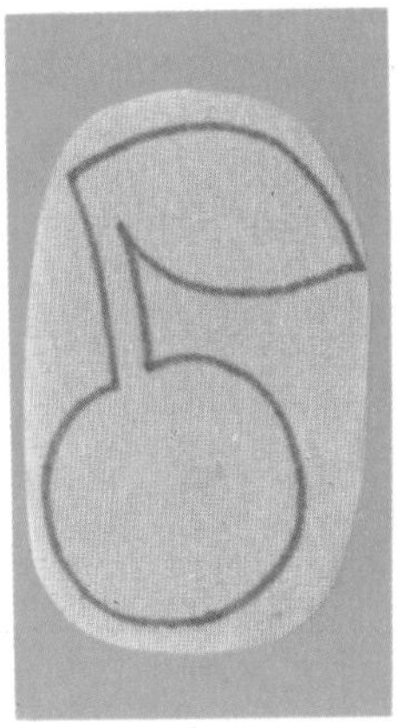

Fig.5a

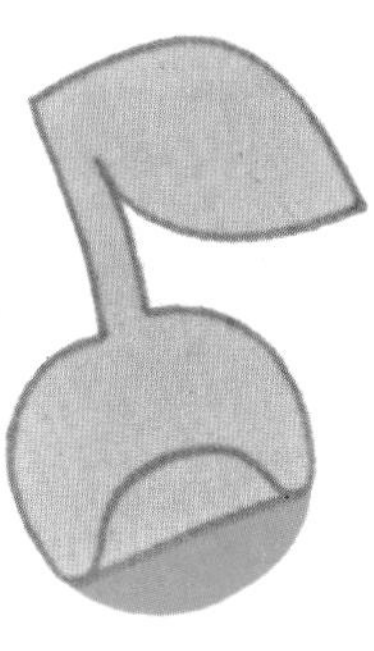

Fig.5b

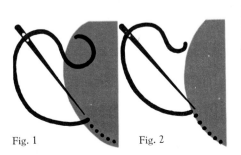

Fig. 1

Fig. 2

fabric and iron into place. Use a steam iron or a dry iron and a damp cloth.

You can then add decorative stitching around the edge. Appliqué bonded in this way will take a lot of wear, but you should add some stitching around the edge to secure pieces if they are to be regularly laundered.

This method is suitable for most fabrics except delicate ones and some, like velvet, which need special care.

Another simple technique is to use a little fabric adhesive on the back of the motif, taking care not to go right up to the edges, then add decorative stitching to secure the edges.

Fraying fabrics

It is not difficult to apply motifs cut from fabrics which fray if a little extra time and trouble is taken in working with one of the methods described here.

Stitch and cut

This is a good method to use on thin fabrics. Cut out a larger area of appliqué fabric than required and mark in the shape of the motif with pencil or chalk.

Baste the motif to the background fabric and work close blanket stitch through both thicknesses around this outline (fig.6). Then carefully cut away the surplus appliqué fabric.

Interfaced method

Another method of dealing with fraying or flimsy fabrics is to reinforce them with iron-on non-woven interfacing before cutting out the exact shape of the motif. This will provide a firm edge on which to work. The motif can then be basted and closely blanket stitched to the background fabric.

Alternatively, cut out the exact shape in the interfacing. Iron it on to a larger piece of the motif fabric, cut out the motif with a seam allowance and apply as for the turned-under method.

Turned-under method

Cut out each appliqué motif, adding hem allowance of 6mm (¼in) all around each shape. Turn in and baste down all raw edges except those which will be overlapped by part of another motif.

If a shape is curved, make snips in the hem allowance at frequent intervals, just less than 6mm (¼in) deep, then turn in the edges (fig.7).

The seam allowance on corners will have to be mitred. To mitre a right-

angled, or wider corner, first fold in one edge then fold over the other and baste (fig.8). To mitre a sharper point, first fold in the point, fold one side over this, then the other and baste to secure (fig.9).

The edges can be pressed lightly before applying, but take care to press only the edge so that the turnings do not mark the right side. Alternatively, baste the shape to the paper pattern and then press the whole piece. The paper will prevent the turnings from marking the right side. Remove basting and paper.

If you are using more than one motif, position each one on the background fabric so that edges which have their hem allowance turned in are placed over those left raw. Pin each motif as it is placed in position, then baste it in place.

The most unobtrusive way of attaching motifs with edges turned under is to use slip stitch. Sew the appliqué neatly in place with small stitches in a matching coloured thread. You could also use small running stitches, blanket stitch or any embroidery stitch.

Appliqué motifs in relief

A pretty variation of appliqué can be achieved by leaving the edges of motifs unattached to the background. For example, flower petals can be attached at the bottom only. Cover the stitches with a separate flower centre slip stitched in place.

Edges of motifs used in this way can be closely blanket stitched to prevent them fraying. Alternatively, they can be cut double, the edges stitched with right sides together, then turned to the outside through a small opening. The opening is then stitched up. The second method takes a little longer to work, but the results are sturdy enough to be used even on children's clothes.

Leaves can also be attached in relief, but stitch these in position with a stem stitched spine, about two thirds the length of the leaf.

If you turn to the photograph on pages 98 and 99 you can see an example of this method. The flower petals and the little boy's hat ribbon, braces and hankie are applied in relief.

With a little thought, you can probably find quite a few motifs in a design which can be treated in this way. Animal's ears or tails and bird's wings are obvious examples, and children especially, love the effect.

Fig. 6 The stitch and cut method. Buttonhole stitching a motif to the background before cutting away the surplus.

Opposite: The photographs of the turned under method show the motif outlined on the fabric ready for cutting out; the final stages of turning under the seam allowance (see fig. 7); and the motif basted to the background fabric so that it can be sewn down.

Fig. 7 The turned under method. The raw edges are turned in and basted down. If the shape is curved, snips should be made in the hem allowance at frequent intervals.
Fig. 8 Mitring a right-angled corner.
Fig. 9 Mitring a corner of less than 90°.

Fig.6

Fig.7

Fig.8

Fig.9

Machine appliqué

Machine-stitched appliqué has the advantage of being hard-wearing, practical for most fabrics and time-saving. Motifs can be reinforced with iron-on, non-woven interfacing in the same way as for hand appliqué.

The stitches

Zigzag, straight and satin stitch are the most common ways of working appliqué on a machine.

Zigzag stitch

If your machine can work a zigzag stitch you will find this invaluable. An open zigzag stitch can be worked round the raw edges of any closely-woven or non-fraying fabric.

Satin stitch

If you close up the zigzag stitch sufficiently you can achieve an effect like fine, smooth satin stitch that can be worked in half the time taken to achieve the same effect by hand. This is ideal for securing and decorating the edges of motifs in one operation.

Satin stitch is best worked with a No.50 sewing thread and a frame to keep the fabric taut. Alternatively,

Right: Sunbonnet Sue and Farmer Boy are two popular appliqué motifs. They are applied with machine zigzag stitch to this continental quilt. The frill on the petticoat is applied in relief – the top of it is stitched to the dress and apron, leaving the bottom edge loose.

Below: A tablemat with sunrise appliqué motifs applied with ric-rac braids; the layers of fabric are placed on top of each other.

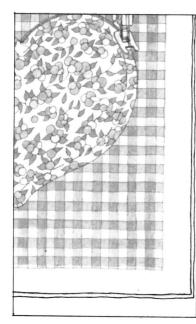

Fig. 1 Working satin stitch by machine. The background fabric, with the motif basted to it, is placed on two sheets of thin paper.
Fig. 2 A motif applied with Russian braid, using a straight machine stitch.
Fig. 3 Russian braid stitched around a motif with zigzag machine stitch.

Right: A colourful rag book with pictures worked in machine appliqué to create a simple story. The motifs were applied onto rectangles of cotton fabric, which were then put together in the correct order. A bonding material [fusible fleece] was used to attach the motifs to the pages.

place the work on two thin sheets of paper when machining to avoid puckering (fig.1). The paper can be easily torn away afterwards.

Before you begin sewing the appliqué it is worthwhile spending some time experimenting with stitch lengths and widths to find the best size satin stitch for a particular fabric. Try loosening the top tension slightly to get the effect you want. Also, practise working very slowly and accurately around angles and curves.

The stitch and cut method, described in the section on hand sewing techniques, works particularly successfully with machine satin stitch.

Straight stitch

Even if your machine does not work a zigzag stitch, there are a number of effective and decorative ways in which you can attach motifs using only a straight stitch.

Unless you are using felt, leather or a non-fraying material, a small turned-under hem must first be basted around the motif.

Edgings

Ric-rac braid provides a quickly worked decorative edge on simple appliqué shapes. Neaten the edges of the shape with open zigzag stitch or oversew [overcast] them by hand and baste to the background.

Baste the ric-rac into position and secure it with straight or zigzag machine stitching down the centre of the braid.

Where ric-rac is used to cover adjacent edges of a motif, these edges should be overlapped by 3mm ($\frac{1}{8}$in) before the ric-rac is basted into place.

Russian braid This is a narrow braid made up of two adjoining cords. It makes a smart alternative edging for motifs. Neaten the edges of the motif as for applying ric-rac braid. Secure the braid with straight stitch worked between the two cords (fig.2) or with open zigzag stitch worked across the cords (fig.3).

Left: The letters on the front and back page were embroidered in stem stitch and the motifs worked with machine zigzag stitch. Felt and embroidered features were added to the chicks and hen.

Above: The correct order of the pages when the book is put together.

Appliqué perse

Appliqué perse is one of the oldest and simplest appliqué techniques. It consists of cutting out a motif from a printed fabric and applying it to the background.

In medieval times, partly worn embroidered or richly patterned fabrics that were too valuable to throw away were cut out and applied to another fabric – thus 'recycling' them.

In the eighteenth century when printed Indian chintz fabrics were the height of fashion, import duty made them prohibitively expensive for most people. So resourceful women carefully cut out each printed motif from scraps of chintz and applied them to lengths of cheaper plain calico.

This 'Persian embroidery', or appliqué perse, as it was known, became a craze. Bedspreads particularly were often decorated with intricate designs made up of carefully arranged printed motifs stitched to a plain background.

Appliqué perse today
Nowadays an infinite variety of printed fabrics are easily available and suitable for appliqué perse. It can be used on most kinds of soft furnishings and looks particularly attractive in a room where you have used a strong pattern on a large area, for example on curtains. The pattern can then be echoed on a smaller area. Appliqué perse can also be used to co-ordinate clothes.

Method of working
If the fabric is likely to fray, add a turning allowance of 6mm ($\frac{1}{4}$in) around the printed outline of the motif. Clip corners and curves and baste the turnings in place before applying the motif.

The easiest patterns to use for appliqué perse are those with a definite motif and a solid outline. If the motif you are using does not have a definite printed outline, you can emphasize it yourself by applying the fabric with an embroidery stitch, machine satin stitch or Russian braid.

You may find it impossible to position a motif of this kind with the straight grain matching the grain of the background. If so, strengthen the motif with iron-on interfacing.

Left: The perse motifs on these velvet cushions have been cut from a fabric which matches the wallpaper, to achieve a co-ordinating furnishing scheme. If you want to buy an expensive print fabric, but can only afford a small amount, this is an ideal way of using it. The technique of appliqué perse can also be used to co-ordinate clothes.

Embroidery & appliqué

Embroidery and appliqué combine naturally together. Basically there are two ways in which you can use embroidery with your appliqué designs – either to stitch down motifs in a decorative way, or to add fine details and extra decoration after working the appliqué.

Any embroidery stitch or technique can be included in an appliqué design. Some of the more common methods are described here, but a good embroidery book will illustrate literally hundreds more stitches.

How much embroidery to include with appliqué is a matter of personal choice and design. But it is important to consider how the finished appliqué will be used. Lavish embroidery will not stand up to hard wear and machine washing; it needs to be hand washed and ironed with care.

However, simple embroidery, if the threads and stitches are carefully chosen, will stand as much wear as the appliqué. Choose firmly twisted cotton thread, like pearl cotton, rather than a stranded or floss cotton, as the individual strands are very fine and split easily. You can use wool yarn, but check that it will stand up to the same sort of washing as the appliqué.

Work firm, compact embroidery stitches, like stem, chain or blanket stitch, rather than more complicated ones that leave a long thread on the surface of the work.

When it comes to more luxurious appliqué or picture making, embroidery can be as lavish and varied as you like to make it.

Applying with embroidery stitches

Blanket stitch is the commonest embroidery stitch used to sew down motifs. It gives the motif a firm edge and if it is closely worked, it can be used to apply woven fabrics without turning under the raw edges. Closely worked satin stitch can be used in the same way.

However, if you want to use any other embroidery stitch to edge a motif cut from woven fabric, you should first secure the appliqué by any one of the unobtrusive hand or machine methods, then add the embroidery.

Some stitches you could use to outline appliqué motifs include: chain stitch, Cretan stitch, feather stitch or stem stitch. Coral stitch, which creates a line of small knots, is an attractive textured stitch.

Couching

Couching is especially useful for working bold outlines, although it will not wash and should be worked in a frame. You can couch down any thread from fine gold thread to cord or string. Secure it at the back of the work and draw it through to the other side. Then catch it at intervals using a small stitch and fine thread.

Cording

Cording, or trailing, makes a bolder raised outline, although it too will not wash and should be worked in a frame. Depending on how thick you want the cord to be, you can use a bundle of embroidery threads, cord or string for the core.

Secure the cord on the wrong side of the work, bring it through to the right side, then cover it with closely worked stitches, coming up and going down almost in the same holes so that the cord is completely invisible.

Applying embroidery and needlepoint

You can easily cut out embroidered pieces of fabric and apply them in the same way as any other fabric, although it is wise to check first that the embroidery will be able to stand up to the same wear as the rest of the appliqué. Also check that the straight grain of the embroidered fabric will run in the same direction as the grain of the background. If not, strengthen the appliqué with iron-on interfacing.

In medieval appliqué, details like faces and hands were often worked in silk on fine needlepoint canvas which was then applied. Mary Queen of Scots used this technique to make many hangings and curtains by applying needlepoint motifs to velvet then edging them with gold thread. In this way, finely detailed motifs could be worked on the canvas, but there was no need to fill in large areas of the background fabric.

Opposite: The Fire of London – a machine embroidered picture, based on a seventeenth century engraving of the Great Fire. The appliquéd fabric is worked over richly with cotton yarn and occasional gold and silver threads. The picture shows musicians escaping from the flames, carrying their instruments to safety.

If you enjoy doing needlepoint, you may like to try this ancient but very simple method of combining appliqué with embroidery. A needlepoint motif, whether it is bold or finely worked has a rich texture that can add something extra to cloth appliqué. It is especially suitable for use with rich fabrics like velvet, brocade and satin although it can also be combined with any textured fabrics. You could, for example, apply richly coloured motifs to a plain velvet dress; or create a simple landscape picture in tweeds and corduroy with a few details, like animals or foliage, in needlepoint.

Worked canvas is a fairly heavy fabric, so you may have to mount the background fabric first.

To apply a needlepoint motif First unravel the canvas up to the embroidery. Pin and baste the canvas in position on the background. With a large-eyed needle take each canvas thread through to the wrong side of the background fabric. Turn to the wrong side and knot the threads together in pairs, pulling so that the canvas is held snugly in place.

The canvas can be outlined with couching, cording or an embroidery stitch, or it can be left plain.

Below: A detail from the Gemini panel – one of the panels of the zodiac quilt on pages 124 and 125. The outlines of the stems, leaves and girl's bonnet are embroidered with stem stitch; the hands, feet and flowers are finished in blanket stitch.

Appliqué on fine fabric

Most appliqué creates a bold solid effect with its contrasts of colours and textures. However, by using sheer, filmy fabrics like chiffon, organdie, batiste, net or lace you can create designs that are shadowed, soft and subtle.

These filmy fabrics are so light-weight and delicate that they are often too fiddly to sew by hand and likely to pucker when sewn by machine using the usual methods.

It is possible, however, to apply them just as successfully as other heavier fabrics, as the photographs in this section illustrate.

Below: A flower spray in shadow appliqué, which has been worked by applying scarlet lawn to white organdie. In some areas the scarlet lawn is on the wrong side of the fabric, giving a soft pink effect; in others it is applied to the right side giving a brilliant contrast.

Shadow appliqué

This is done by basting another piece of the background fabric to the wrong side of the transparent background, outlining the design with stitchery and finally cutting away the excess fabric on the back of the work.

The finished effect is of a solid area of design surrounded by a filmy background.

Shadow appliqué is ideal for delicate curtains, special tablecloths, bedspreads, lingerie or baby clothes.

The background fabric should be

fine enough to allow the fabric applied on the back to show through on the front of the work.

You can work the appliqué using another piece of the background, or you could use a fabric with a different texture but in the same colour, for example, white satin on white organdie. Alternatively, you could use a coloured fabric for the appliqué – red lawn applied to the back of white organdie will show through on the right side of the work as a soft pink. You could also work some parts of the appliqué on the front so that the finished design would be in white, pink and red.

Method of working

Using this method you can create very fine intricate designs because the stitching is worked first, then the excess fabric is cut away. You do not have to worry about cutting tiny shapes out of the delicate fabric or turning under raw edges.

Transfer the design to the right side of the background fabric. You will usually be able to do this simply by laying the fabric over the design. Then trace directly onto the fabric with tailors' chalk or use a hard pencil to draw a very fine line.

Take a piece of the appliqué fabric, which should be larger all round than the design or motif, and baste it to the wrong side of the background fabric.

Now turn to the right side and stitch around the outline of the design through both layers of fabric. You should use a fine thread suitable for weight of the fabric – twisted silk, two strands of embroidery cotton or sewing thread.

There are two different sewing methods.

Backstitch method Work a line of neat backstitch along the lines of the design. You can, if you wish, reinforce the backstitch with a more decorative stitch like chain stitch, coral knot stitch or by couching down a slightly thicker thread (fig.1).

Pin stitch method Basically this is a drawn fabric stitch, but it makes a strong neat finish on delicate appliqué. The finished effect is of a series of openwork holes made by pulling the fabric firmly with a fine thread. These holes become dominant and the connecting stitches almost invisible.

To work pin stitch (figs.2a and 2b), secure the thread on the wrong side of the work, turn to the right side and bring the needle through both layers at A. Insert the needle at B and bring it out at C. Insert the needle again at B, bringing it out at C. Insert the needle once more at B and bring it out at D. Repeat these steps, pulling each stitch firmly.

On the back of the work, remove the

Left: Fine, filmy fabrics can be applied as successfully as stronger fabrics if the motifs are cut and sewn carefully. This appliqué tablecloth was made by basting pieces of fabric on the wrong side of the background fabrics and outlining them with stitches in the shapes of the motifs. The excess fabric on the back of the work was then cut away.

Fig. 1 The backstitch method. Reinforcing the backstitch by couching down a slightly thicker thread.
Fig. 2 The pin stitch method.

Fig.1

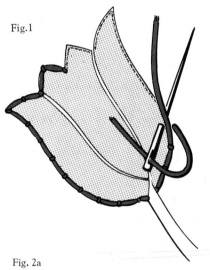

Fig. 2a

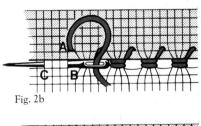

Fig. 2b

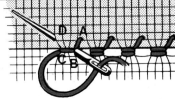

Above: Two different types of net have been used to form the main bark and leaf motifs on these delicate net curtains. The shapes can be applied using the lace appliqué method described on this page.

basting stitches and trim away the surplus fabric close to the line of stitching using sharp embroidery scissors to prevent the edge becoming ragged.

Either of these shadow work methods can be used to apply fabric to the front of the background fabric, or to apply more solid fabrics, You can also apply cotton lawn to net, using the decorative backstitch method to make a kind of lace called Carrickmacross lace.

Appliqué with lace

You can easily apply lace or other fine fabrics using a swing needle sewing machine. The work needs to be backed with paper during sewing to prevent it stretching or being puckered by the action of the machine.

Method of working

Cut a piece of lace larger than the motif required. Draw the motif on paper and baste it on the wrong side of the lace (fig.3). Work a row of straight stitches around the motif outline from the wrong side.

On the right side, work a line of small zigzag stitches over the straight stitches. Cut away the excess lace

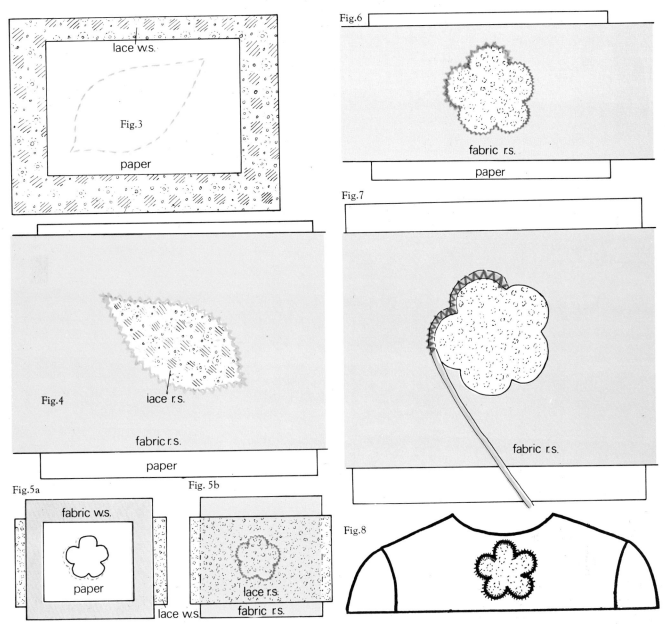

Fig.3

Fig.4

Fig.5a

Fig. 5b

Fig.6

Fig.7

Fig.8

around the motif and remove the paper.

Baste the lace motif to the background fabric. Place another piece of paper beneath the background fabric and work a slightly larger row of zigzag stitches over the first to attach the motif to the background (fig.4). Then, tear away the paper.

Lace insets
Lace insets look very attractive on lingerie or on any delicate clothes, and they are very simple to work.
Method Draw the shape of the inset on a piece of paper. Baste the paper to the wrong side of the background fabric and baste a piece of lace, larger than the motif, to the right side of it.

On the wrong side, work a line of straight stitches around the motif through all the thicknesses. On the

right side, go over the straight stitches with a row of small zigzag stitches (figs. 5a, 5b).

Trim away the excess lace close to the edges of the motif. Trim away the fabric on the wrong side of the lace motif. Tear away the paper.

Place another sheet of paper on the wrong side of the background fabric. On the right side, work a slightly larger line of zigzag stitches over the first (fig.6). Remove the paper.

If the lace is very fine, a permanent backing of fine nylon jersey can be attached in the same way as the paper. This gives the lace extra strength without loosing transparency.

If you cannot work zigzag stitch, you can work two rows of straight stitch or backstitch close together around the motif. Then go over the outline with couching or a decorative embroidery stitch as a finishing touch (figs.7, 8).

Fig. 3 Applying lace. Straight stitches worked around the motif shape from the wrong side.
Fig. 4 Attaching the motif to the background with zigzag stitches.
Figs. 5a, 5b Lace inserts. Paper basted to the wrong side, and lace basted to the right side, of the background fabric.
Fig. 6 Zigzag stitches worked over the straight stitches on the right side.
Fig. 7 When zigzag stitch cannot be used, couching can be worked over rows of straight stitch or backstitch.
Fig. 8 Lace inserts add interest and individuality to dresses and blouses.

111

Cut paper appliqué

Making appliqué from paper cut-outs is one of the simplest and most enjoyable ways of planning a design. In the eighteenth century there was a craze for cut paper novelties, and women applied designs that had been cut from folded paper by their friends, children and sweethearts.

When American missionaries went to Hawaii they taught the island women their sewing skills, which included patchwork and the fashionable cut paper appliqué. The island women quickly developed a very individual way of making appliqué quilts. They adapted the idea of paper cut-outs to mirror the lush natural life of their islands. Their motifs, first

Fig. 1

Fig. 2

Fig. 3

drawn onto folded paper, included breadfruit, pumpkins, pawpaws, figs, ferns, turtles and waterfalls. They had no need to save scraps of cloth in the way that the American women had, so their designs developed into huge flowing patterns that were often so big that they covered the whole quilt.

Motifs were usually red or green on a white background. Red and yellow, the traditional royal colours used in their emperors' feather cloaks, were often combined.

Quilting was worked in equally spaced lines following the contours of the appliqué motif. This was called *luma-lau*, or wave quilting.

A host of rules and conventions grew up around the making of these quilts. It was forbidden for anyone but the artist herself to sit on a quilt while it was being stitched. Designs had to be original, plagiarism was frowned on and was denounced at the next *luau*, the public gathering.

Method of working
There are many ways of using cut paper appliqué. Motifs can be applied to quilt blocks, cushion covers, clothes and furnishings. A chain of little people, each appliquéd in a different print could edge a child's dress or a denim skirt. A row of palm trees or fir trees could march across a skyline in a simple picture appliqué. You could cut snowflakes out of a variety of textured white fabrics, apply them to a blue background and add pearls and white sequins for a glamourous winter picture.

Fabrics for this type of appliqué should have a firm, close weave like lawn or poplin, or you could use felt which needs no turnings.

Designs are made from squares of paper, folded twice or four times, then cut in exactly the same way that children make snowflakes and doillies. In fact, children will probably love to make some of the designs. This is an ideal way of making an appliqué for a child from his or her own design, or of commemorating some special family occasion.

Drawing the design
Draw the design onto the folded paper first if you want to make something like an animal or a leaf, or just cut straight into the paper. Unfold the paper to see how the design is developing and refold it to make more cuts if necessary.

Make the squares of paper fairly large, about 15cm to 20.5cm (6in to 8in), and the designs bold. Tiny intricate shapes will be difficult to stitch down. You can cut really large designs from folded sheets of newspaper.

You can also make corner designs from folded triangles and borders from folded strips of paper. A simple zigzag or palm tree design is easy to cut from a folded strip, so are the chains of people that children enjoy cutting out.

Transferring the design
Unfold the cut paper, lay it on the fabric and trace off the design. For woven fabrics, add 6mm (¼in) all round the edge and clip angles and curves. Baste the motif down to the background fabric. Cut out the designs in the centre of the motif using small sharp scissors. Leave enough seam allowance to turn under and clip the angles. Sew the motif down using slip stitch or any decorative stitch.

Opposite: A detail from a nineteenth century Hawaiian quilt, in which different prints have been used for the repeating motifs. The shapes for this Snowflake design were cut from folded paper (figs. 1-3).

Fig. 1 Use a square of paper which will be long enough, when folded, to accomodate your pattern. Fold the square in half, and then in half again. The quarter square formed should then be folded diagonally into a triangle.

Fig. 2 On the folded triangle draw cutting lines as indicated. Cut evenly along these lines through all the layers.

Fig. 3 Unfold the pattern pieces and pin them to the fabric you have chosen, adding a 6mm (¼in) seam allowance around each piece.

Left: A concertina fold design.

Ribbon appliqué

Applying ribbon to simply cut clothes and soft furnishings is a very effective way of adding a luxury look; a plain skirt can be given a dramatic border of ribbons of different widths and textures in toning colours; an ordinary plain fabric evening bag can be decorated with three-dimensional ribbon flowers; or a cushion can be trimmed with a 'lightning flash' as shown in the photograph.

Alternatively, this technique can be used for a practical purpose; for example, a child's outgrown dress can be given months more life by letting down the hem and covering any line with a pretty embroidered ribbon.

There are basically two ways of applying ribbon – flat onto the background or by folding and knotting to make a three-dimensional pattern.

Choose a closely woven fabric or felt to work on.

Applying ribbon flat

Choose a simple design based on straight lines. For ideas, look through books on Art Deco or primitive art, they will contain plenty of angular designs that can quite easily be adapted and copied for Ribbon appliqué.

Look at the two cushions on page 116. The lightning flash on one achieves its impact from the use of different textures and widths of ribbon. The basket effect on the other is achieved by stitching three ribbons together with a close machine zigzag

Opposite: A striking idea for a bedspread and matching wall panel, using brightly coloured ribbon appliqué.

Left: Ribbon appliqué looks very attractive on clothes. Velvet ribbon has been applied around the cuffs and top hem of this romantic evening dress.

stitch and then interweaving them before stitching into position on the background. The basket weave method could be continued across the whole cushion, or used on the bodice or yoke of a dress.

Plan your design on paper first and transfer the outlines to the background fabric. Pin and baste the ribbon into place, make folds and mitre the

excess on corners as shown (figs.1a, 1b).

Sew the ribbon down with straight or zigzag machine stitch or backstitch by hand. You could add a line of embroidery in a wide, open stitch, like chain or herringbone, if you want a narrow line to follow the design. The folds can be slip stitched or back-stitched by hand with small stitches.

Ribbons can also be applied one on

top of another, using a narrower ribbon each time, to add another dimension to your design.

Three-dimensional use of ribbon

Interesting results can be produced by knotting, folding and plaiting ribbon in a variety of ways before stitching it to a background. This type of appliqué is suitable for picture making and for luxury items such as evening clothes which do not receive hard wear.

The work can be as simple or elaborate as you wish, or as your dexterity will allow. Start with the ideas shown here and then experiment with your own.

Petersham [grosgrain] is suitable for this work as it holds a shape well and is relatively easy to handle. Details can be added to the ribbon with embroidery stitches or beads.

Unless you are using embroidery stitches, when you stitch folded ribbon into place, the stitches should be sufficient to hold the ribbon securely, but they should be unobtrusive. Do not add too many stitches or you will find that they will flatten the motif.

Fig. 1a

Fig. 1b

Figs. 1a, 1b Baste the ribbon into place and cut off excess fabric to form a mitred corner.

Left, above: The braid flowers in this appliqué picture have been made by looping the braid into individual petals and securing them with several stitches. Double loops worked either side of a centre line form the ears of corn [wheat].

Left, below: Some examples of the three-dimensional use of ribbon: a simple flower, made by folding ribbon and trimming it with beads; a scroll formed from coiled ribbon; a criss-crossed velvet ribbon stitched to petersham [grosgrain]; and a chevron design made up before being stitched in place.

San Blas appliqué

San Blas or mola work – appliqué in reverse – is worked with great skill by the Cuna Indian women of the San Blas Islands, which are off the coast of Panama.

In the 1880's when missionaries and traders came into contact with the Cuna Indians, they turned from body painting to making 'molas' or bright multi-coloured cloth panels covered with designs.

At first mola meant the cotton

Right: A San Blas islander displaying her work. This kind of appliqué is traditionally used to decorate molas, the short sleeved blouses which are important status symbols on the islands.

blouses worn by the women. Early molas were simple, made only of dark blue material with a single narrow band of coloured fabric around the bottom. The band gradually became wider and more intricate in design. When traders brought brighter coloured fabric to the islands, the designs became even more elaborate, involving up to five or six layers of fabric in as many colours.

San Blas design

The primitive and gay designs reflect life on the islands and many are based on plants, animals and people. Some designs are entirely geometric and non-representational while others show demons and monsters from Indian lore. Contemporary life is mirrored in the motifs of the molas; design elements from advertisements and famous people, like soccer players and astronauts, have all appeared in molas.

The Cunas seem to abhor a vacuum so they fill the entire surface with design. Slits, dots, sawtooth lines and

Below: Primitive stylized animals and trees are the subjects of this piece of mola work. The appliqué is combined with simple embroidery for finer detail.

other simple and small designs will fill up any area not covered by the main motif. The resulting fabric, so completely filled with design, is very durable and has a quilted effect.

This appliqué technique is ideal for fashion where rich bold effects are required. It would be striking worked as a border around the bottom of a skirt or evening cloak, or as pockets and yoke on a smock. A small waistcoat lavishly worked in San Blas appliqué would be warm and very decorative. On curtains, cushion covers, bedspreads and wall hangings mola appliqué would look particularly dramatic.

Method of working

This appliqué technique is more a method of cutting away than applying pieces of fabric. Several layers of different coloured fabrics are placed together, then parts of the top layers of fabric are cut away to reveal a section of the colour below.

Five layers at the most are workable, but experiment with two or three layers of fabric to start with, and introduce any extra colour by pushing small pieces of fabric into holes in the design. On large articles, such as a skirt, where working with several layers would be impossible, pieces of fabric can be appliquéd in the traditional way – then the small areas within cut away and neatened.

When cutting out the design always cut out shapes smaller than their finished size to allow for the turnings, which are folded under and stitched down.

Choose lightweight fabrics with a firm, close weave such as cotton poplin or lawn. Heavy fabrics will fray more easily and the turnings will be bulky. Felt, however, requires no turnings so is particularly well suited to cushions and similar objects.

Basic technique

To understand the basic technique, read through the step by step instructions for this simple bird motif.

Take four pieces of fabric about 15cm (6in) square and in strong contrasting colours. Baste the four layers together, one on top of the other and right side up.

Trace the design onto tracing paper and cut out a separate trace pattern for each colour.

On the top fabric, draw around the outside shape and, allowing about 3mm ($\frac{1}{8}$in) for turnings, cut out using sharp pointed scissors. Clip into

Opposite: A bird motif which has been adapted from a Mexican pattern. It is well suited to San Blas appliqué and provides an ideal practice-ground for beginners to this technique.

Below left: Layers of fabric basted together, with part of the top layer slip stitched around the motif outline, revealing a blue layer underneath.

Below right: A cross has been cut in the last circle to expose the pupil of the eye. The turnings are being slip stitched under.

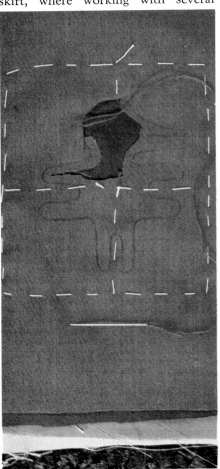

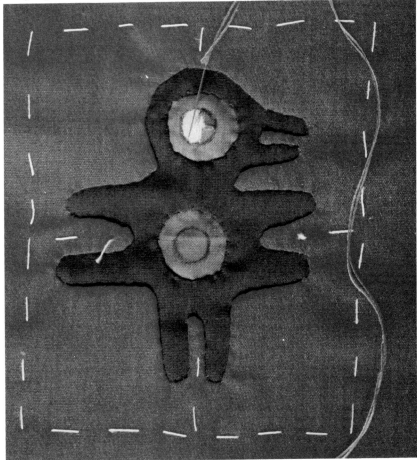

points and around curves so that the turnings lie flat.

Fold under the turnings, and if necessary, pin and baste. Work slip stitch or running stitch around the edges, taking the thread through all the layers of fabric.

If you cut through a layer by mistake it is easy to repair by inserting a scrap of fabric of the same colour into the slit and stitching the folded edges to it.

Two colours are now exposed, the top layer and the second. You are now ready to cut through to expose the third layer of material.

Trace the outline for the third layer, the iris of the bird's 'eyes', onto the second layer.

Cut away the second layer to within 3mm ($\frac{1}{8}$in) of the outline. Turn the edges under and stitch down as before.

Three layers of fabric are now exposed. Repeat the process to expose the fourth and final layer. Cutting away the layers one by one like this is a simple form of reverse appliqué.

Variations

There are however more sophisticated variations of this technique. Instead of cutting all the way through to the base layer you can leave some shapes with only the second or third colour exposed. Or, if you want the third colour only to show, you can by-pass the second layer by slightly lifting the top layer and snipping the second layer far enough back so that it does not show.

Alternatively, you can cut openings in the top fabric and push small pieces of different coloured fabrics underneath the top layer and stitch down turnings.

You can also stitch other colours down on top in the traditional surface appliqué method.

San Blas is a rewarding form of needlework that can be more intriguing and challenging than surface appliqué. Variations on the basic technique are almost limitless and there are great possibilities for experimenting with colours and shapes.

Below: A colourful tablemat with a Cuna bird motif in reverse appliqué, using three layers of fabric.

Chapter 7
Appliqué in the home

Appliqué on furnishings

Right: A beautiful quilt which
features all the signs of the zodiac.
Details of two panels are on
pages 89 and 106. Although
a large item takes time to complete,
a well designed quilt is a very
worthwhile project. It will form a
focal point in a bedroom and can be
kept for years as a family heirloom.

You can use appliqué almost everywhere in the home. It is such a quick
and simple way of covering large areas
of fabric and there is nothing more
satisfying than knowing that you have
turned an everyday item into something unique and attractive.

Appliqué is also an economical way
of achieving that fashionable and

Above: The motifs on this treasure island tablecloth were worked on a sewing machine. The shapes were appliquéd to the background with a close zigzag stitch, giving them a bold, firm outline.

expensive co-ordinated look in home furnishings. If you make up a pair of curtains you can use the left-over scraps of fabric to work simple motifs on cushion covers or a tablecloth in the same room. You can also work a motif on a large scale on a quilt or tablecloth, then apply smaller motifs, or parts of the design, to other furnishings in the same room.

Before you appliqué any item of home furnishing, do consider how it will be washed. A tablecloth or continental quilt cover, for instance, should be able to stand up to a weekly wash. Make sure that all the fabrics you use on any one article can stand up to the same type of washing, whether it is a hot machine wash or a cool hand wash.

Also, make sure that the straight grain of the motifs matches the grain of the background fabric, and that the appliqué pieces are sewn down securely enough to stand up to the type of washing and wear they will receive.

Method of working

Ideally, for any article that will be regularly machine washed, you should use the turned-under method of preparing the appliqué, whether sewing by hand or machine. This method gives motifs a firm non-fraying edge. It is worth the small amount of extra time involved, as there is nothing more

annoying than having to secure loose fraying edges every time the appliqué comes out of the wash.

Most of the items you make for the home will be too large for the appliqué to be worked in an embroidery frame. So you should keep the background fabric flat, spread on a table or the floor, while pinning and basting the motifs. Baste them down more securely than you would if working in a frame.

If you are sewing the appliqué by machine, roll up the fabric tightly to pass under the arm (fig.1).

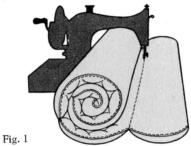

Fig. 1

Fig. 1 If you are making a large item and using a machine to apply motifs or stitch seams, you should roll up the fabric tightly so that it can pass under the arm.

Left: A practical and decorative Noah's Ark quilt. Some of the motifs have been applied with zigzag stitch; others with blanket stitch.

Picture making with appliqué

Making appliqué pictures is tremendous fun. You can let your imagination run riot, indulge yourself in the pleasure of colours and textures and spend many hours absorbed in a creative activity that can be as straightforward or as complicated as you like to make it.

You can include any fabric and an endless variety of of other materials and objects in a picture, anything in fact, that you can sew to a background fabric can become part of a picture.

Do not confuse appliqué, where materials are sewn down, with collage where they are stuck to a background. You can easily combine the two, but stitchery in some form or other is an important and integral part of the effect created by an appliqué picture.

Stitchery

Stitchery can be restricted to the way in which motifs are sewn down, or it can be lavish and elaborate. The detail of an Egyptian-style hanging shows how even the very simplest stitching can create a lively and successful primitive effect entirely in harmony with the design and the materials.

In other pictures, the appliqué stitches are obscured completely by embroidery or worked boldly.

Be aware of the very different effects that are created by each method of sewing down appliqué. Look through this book or make a sampler. Cut out a shape a number of times from the same fabric and then apply each motif using a different method. Some methods, like couching or satin stitch, give a heavy raised outline; others like slip stitch give a softer one.

For a really crisp outline, you can apply shapes over a card template, leaving the card in the finished work. For a very soft, feathered outline, you can stitch a motif down just inside the edge and fray the raw edges up to the stitching.

Below: An Egyptian-style hanging in soft, muted colours which combines appliqué and embroidery. Hessian [burlap] was chosen as the background fabric and the motifs were applied by the turned under method.

Left: A detail from the hanging, showing how embroidery stitches have been used to add detail to the motifs.

Above: A variety of fabrics and household items have been used in these delightful lion and tiger appliqué pictures. The main shapes have been cut from felt and wool fabric; the shading on the bodies from net. Beads, curtain rings, leather, string and raffia have been used for the animal features and the cornfield.

Try to work pictures in a frame big enough to take the whole design, or a large section of it, at one time. Not only will the frame make it easier to use a wide range of techniques, including couching and cording, but it will also make it easier to add to the design as you go along, laying new fabrics and threads down so that you can see the overall effect.

Designing pictures

Some people let a collection of fabrics inspire a design; others work out a design first and then choose suitable fabrics. Some people like to plan a design in detail down to the last stitch, while others cut shapes directly from fabric and build up a design as they go along. Planning a picture, choosing shapes, colours and textures is an entirely individual matter. Be fairly flexible at the beginning, use your design to help you select suitable fabrics, and allow the fabrics you have available to shape the design.

The chapter on general appliqué design suggests various ways in which you can build up pictures from photographs and illustrations, and ways in which you can create abstract designs.

Decide roughly on the overall size of your picture and draw your design, keeping the appliqué shapes fairly large and simple in outline. Do not bother to colour in your design, except to indicate general colour areas, as you will never be able to match the fabric exactly to paints or crayons. Instead, keep a pile of possible appliqué fabrics near as you draw, or spread them around the finished outline drawing, so that you will be aware not only of colour, but of the textures and patterns of the fabrics.

Remember that some motifs can be made more prominent by padding or stuffing (see page 133). Be aware also that colours can be softened and contrasts blurred by applying net or transparent fabrics over solid colours.

Look at your design to see if it forms a balanced whole; note the shapes of the exposed background areas to see how they contribute to the picture.

At this stage you should consider how the picture will be displayed. Will the appliqué go right up to the edges of the picture or will it be surrounded by background fabric; if so, how much space should you leave around the appliqué so that the whole design is balanced? Will the picture have a border in another fabric or will it be framed? Will it be mounted over a board or left as a soft hanging? You need not decide until the picture is finished, but bear these questions in mind as they will affect the design.

Do not try to include too many things in one picture. You will probably enjoy using picture making

Below: A village scene, in which the details have been picked out with embroidery and appliqué. The picture was first outlined on canvas and a light wash painted for the sky and distant hills. The main appliqué shapes were outlined in cable stitch and French knots. Felt was introduced for the chimney pots and the clock to provide strong outlines.

131

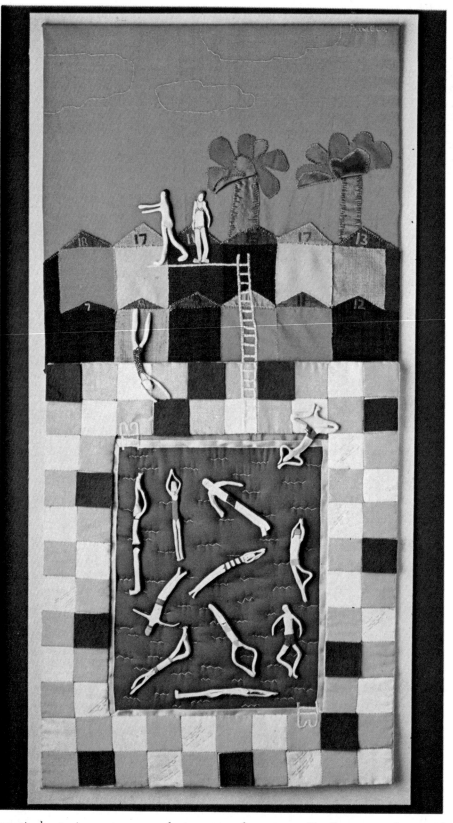

creatively, trying out new techniques or new stitches, but beware of getting carried away and trying to cram in every fabric, stitch or technique that appeals to you.

Fabrics – colours and textures

The background fabric is the largest piece of fabric you will need; its colour and texture will affect your choice of appliqué fabrics.

It should have a firm, close weave and should be heavy enough to take the weight of all the appliqué. If it is not very strong, or if you are making something large, it can be backed with calico [unbleached muslin] and the two fabrics treated as one. Be sure that the background fabric is large enough to include any turnings or seam allowances necessary for finishing and displaying the picture.

A large collection of fabrics is a great inspiration for picture making. Choosing the right fabric for each motif is one of the most enjoyable aspects of picture making. Try to select fabrics in daylight; pick them up, hold them against each other and lay them on the background fabric to see how the colours and textures combine. Do the same with embroidery thread, ribbon, cord or any other decoration you might use.

Be selective and ruthlessly discard anything that does not contribute to the picture. Look at the pictures shown here and see how each fabric is used selectively and creatively. You will see that a wide variety of fabrics are used overall, but that in each picture the fabrics are very carefully chosen. In the kneeling knight panel, for example, all the textures are very rich although the range of colours is limited. The gold satin, brocade, lame and silver kid all work together and enhance the stylized heraldic design.

In the lion picture (below) the main motif has been cut from corduroy, which has been used so that it gives a three-dimensional effect. Purple felt has been used for the background.

Padded appliqué

There are many occasions when you may want to emphasize a shape by raising or padding it. The technique is particularly useful for picture making, but it can be used on clothes and home furnishings too.

There are two different methods to choose from.

Method 1 gives a slightly raised domed effect. The padding is made up of several layers of felt in graduating sizes.

Use the paper template to cut as many pieces of felt as you need; three layers will slightly raise a motif enough to emphasise it on clothes, six or more layers will create a really domed shape.

Cut the first layer 6mm ($\frac{1}{4}$in) smaller all round than the edge of the motif. The succeeding layers should all decrease by 6mm ($\frac{1}{4}$in). Outline the shape of the motif on the background fabric and sew down the smallest piece of felt in the centre of the motif using stab stitches. Apply the other layers in the same way.

Mark the shape on the appliqué fabric and cut it out a fraction outside the mark to allow for stretching.

Below: The clever use of corduroy in this lion picture achieves a three-dimensional effect. The tail and mane were worked in long, straight stitches; the eyes, nose and claws in satin stitch; the whiskers in French knots and the outline of the tail in back stitch.

Overleaf: The design of this kneeling knight panel was inspired by the medieval brasses found in churches. The rich fabrics have been well chosen to suit the subject. Gold thread, silver kid and metal waste provide interesting and unusual detail. Parts of the picture have been padded – a useful technique for picture making.

Method 2 Cut out the appliqué motif, making it very slightly larger all round than its finished size on the design, so that when it is sewn down a 'bubble' is formed in the centre which will be filled with stuffing. Leave enough of the edge unstitched so that you can push a padding of cotton wool or kapok between the background and the appliqué fabric. Push the padding in with the points of your scissors or a bodkin.

This method of padding can create a really high raised area, especially if the padding is firmly pushed in. Sew down the opening to complete the work.

Preparing for display

A picture can be finished off for display in a number of ways.

Mounting is simple to do and provides a firm backing and a sharp outline. Take a piece of plywood cut exactly to the required finished size of the panel. Lay the board centrally over the back of the work. Then with fine string or strong linen thread, lace the fabric (not too near the edge) at the back from side to side and from top to bottom Then, pull the lacing firmly so that the work is evenly stretched without being puckered. Secure the lacing threads by knotting several times.

Neaten the back by stitching calico, or felt, over it to conceal the lacing. Take the backing fabric, and turn under the edges 12mm (½in) all around (felt does not need any turnings). Next, baste and then slip stitch firmly in place to cover the lacing. Remove the basting threads.

You can then frame the picture if you wish. Alternatively, stitch two curtain rings to the back on either side about half-way down to hold a cord for hanging the panel on a wall.

Cotton or felt backing If you prefer a softer finish for a large hanging, it can simply be backed with cotton or felt. Turn under the raw edges of the picture to the size required and baste. Cut a piece of backing fabric and turn under the raw edges to the same size as the picture. Baste, and slip stitch the two together. You can then sew curtain rings on the back along the top of the picture and hang it up from hooks.

Alternatively, you can make loops from pieces of the background fabric, stitch these along the top of the picture at the back and slide a length of dowel or curtain rod through the loops.

You can also turn in the sides of the picture to make casings along the top and bottom for dowel.

Chapter 8
Fashion appliqué

Appliqué on clothes

Appliqué can give mass-produced clothes an exclusive, individual touch, as well as making simple home-made clothes special and stylish. It can liven up a dull wardrobe, co-ordinate separates and make casual clothes lively and fun, as the photographs on the following pages illustrate.

Even the simplest appliqué motif makes a garment individual and unique to its owner. Motifs can be as simple as a single flower or an elaborate design covering the whole garment.

Planning fashion appliqué
Before you reach for your scissors, you must choose your fabrics very carefully, and make some preliminary decisions about design and decoration.

Fabrics
The fabrics you use for fashion appliqué will depend on the style of your clothes, the type of design and current fashion. But clothes are things that you feel and touch as you wear them, so be aware of the different textures that can be used for this kind of appliqué. Fashion impact often depends on texture as much as design. For example satin makes a smooth contrast against velvet or cotton; heavily-textured fabrics like tweed, corduroy or suede make an exciting contrast when applied to smooth jersey or denim.

Consider the wash- and wearing-ability of fabrics before you begin the appliqué. For instance, you may have to decide whether it is worth turning a washable garment into one that must be dry cleaned because the fabric you intend to apply is not washable.

Be aware also of the relative weight and strength of the fabrics you want to use. If you want to apply a heavy fabric to a lighter one, suede on jersey for example, then you must be prepared to mount the background fabric (see page 27) before working the appliqué, so that it can take the extra weight. If you do not, then the appliqué may cause the garment to sag and hang out of shape.

If you are applying a light fabric to a heavier one, say silk on denim, strengthen the appliqué fabric with iron-on interfacing.

Decoration
You can add all sorts of decoration to fashion appliqué. Motifs can be highlighted with embroidery or beads and sequins. You could work the appliqué using cord, ribbon or braid to outline a design or to link motifs.

Again, decide whether these additions will affect the wash- and wearing-ability of the finished garment. Most beads and sequins can be hand washed if they are securely sewn on, but check first by washing a sample. Heavily beaded garments should be dry cleaned. Any ribbons or braids that will be washed should be washed before applying to check for shrinkage and to test that they are colourfast.

Design
Appliqué design on clothes depends as much on current fashion as on personal choice. But a design should also suit the style of the garment. When planning an appliqué design on clothes, try to imagine the garment as a whole with the appliqué forming an important, but complementary, decoration.

Decide where you will position appliqué motifs. A garment may have obvious features that you can highlight with appliqué – a yoke or bodice panel, patch pockets, cuffs, sleeves or skirt are obvious choices depending on the style.

You can also use appliqué to draw attention to, or draw the eye away from, good or bad features. For instance, you can show off pretty legs with an appliqué skirt border or create a slimming effect with a vertical design. Remember, the appliqué will probably be the first thing people will notice so use it to your best advantage.

Home dressmaking
When you are choosing a pattern with appliqué in mind, keep to simple styles with a minimum of seaming detail. Appliqué cannot be worked successfully over pleats or gathers. It is a bold form of decoration, so do not force it to compete with all sorts of other details. The more appliqué you are going to work on a garment, the simpler the style should be. Try to visualize the finished garment, with

Opposite: Appliqué at its most romantic. In these dresses traditional techniques have been adapted to modern design concepts. The blue organza apron is applied with field flowers, and surface embroidery has been added to enrich the design. The black bodice and sleeves of the lilac dress are applied with flowers and leaves of machine embroidered organza, and realistic-looking plastic blackberries.

Right: Swallow motifs, in a printed fabric, transform this simple long skirt into an interesting and individual garment. The bold outlines of the bird motifs make them easy to apply, either with satin or zigzag stitch.

Opposite: Appliqué is an ideal way to brighten up a pair of jeans and make them unique. Printed and plain fabrics have been combined with beads and embroidery stitches. The herringbone stitch on the pocket of the jeans has been echoed on the jacket to co-ordinate the outfit.

Overleaf: An appliquéd hood and muff which are perfect accessories for a winter wedding dress. The ivy leaf motifs are joined by tendrils worked in zigzag stitch.

its appliqué, when you are choosing the pattern.

When you have chosen your pattern, decide exactly where the appliqué will go. Will it be worked entirely on one pattern piece, or will it have to cover any seams? Make a tracing of each relevant pattern piece and draw the design on it. If the design is to go over any seams, stick the traced pattern pieces together to draw the final design. When you have decided on the design, trace it off and cut out the shapes to use as templates.

If possible, you should work the appliqué before making up the garment so that you are working on a flat piece of fabric which is less likely to pucker.

If the design is to be worked on one pattern piece, outline the pattern shape and the appliqué design on the fabric but do not cut out the pattern. Frame the fabric if you wish and work the appliqué. Check the outlines of the pattern piece in case the appliqué has caused the outlines to distort at all. This is more likely to happen if you have included a lot of embroidery.

If the appliqué covers any seams, study the pattern instructions carefully to decide at what stage in making up the garment you should add the appliqué. Always aim to work appliqué on a background that can be spread flat.

For instance, if the appliqué is to go all round a four-panel skirt, sew the panels together but leave the centre back seam unstitched.

If the appliqué is to be worked near any hem, on a skirt, sleeve or smock, always check that the hem is the right length before finally stitching down the appliqué. The appliqué design should appear balanced in relation to the hem.

Avoid working appliqué over any complicated or curving seams, for example a bust dart. Try to adjust your design so that only embroidery is worked over this type of seam.

Appliqué on ready-made clothes

The main problem in working appliqué on ready-made clothes is to ensure that the background is as flat and smooth as possible so that there will be no puckering when the appliqué is finally stitched down.

Depending on where you are positioning the appliqué, you may find it easier to put the garment on a tailor's dummy. Alternatively, try it on yourself and get a friend to pin motifs on for you.

Do pin and baste carefully, checking all the time that there is no puckering of the appliqué or background fabrics.

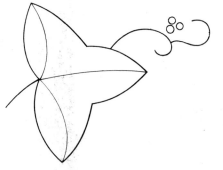

Chapter 9
Appliqué library

The silhouettes of veteran cars make very
good shapes for appliqué pictures. The one
shown here has been cut out in large
simple shapes, which are held in place
with an outline of satin machine
stitching. Details such as the spokes of the
wheel and hand brake have been worked
in varying widths of zigzag stitch. If hand
stitching is preferred, buttonhole and
satin stitches would be suitable for
applying the shapes to the background.

This enchanting appliqué design can be applied by hand, using satin stitch to sew the shapes to the background, and working the details in back stitch, satin stitch and stem stitch. Here machine embroidery has been used, with satin stitch to hold the shapes and free embroidery for the details. The motif is perfect for the nursery on bedspreads, curtains or cushions. It could also be used on toddler's clothes or on a pinafore.

Buttonhole stitch has been worked around
these flower motifs. The clever use of
different shades of fabric creates a realistic
three-dimensional effect. The details on
the flowers and leaves are worked in
stranded cotton, using long and short
stitch, stem stitch, and back stitch.
The stems are double rows of chain stitch.
A design of this size would be suitable for
tablecloth corners, bedroom cushions or
a framed picture.

The stitch and cut method of appliqué has
been used here to create a simple picture in
delicate pastel shades. The shapes are
held down with finely worked buttonhole
stitch. The details of face features, hair,
shoes and buttons are worked in satin
stitch and stem stitch. The background
fabric is of waffle weave cotton and the
applied pieces are fine cotton lawn.
This design would make a pretty
decoration for a cot or pram cover.

145

An example of appliqué perse, which is an
ideal way of co-ordinating furnishing
schemes. This motif was cut from a coarse
linen printed furnishing fabric and
applied to a plain linen background.
Zigzag machine stitching was used to sew
it down, but hand buttonhole stitch could
have been used instead. The veins on these
leaves could be embroidered to bring out
the details in the motif.

This enchanting bouquet of flowers is
worked in appliqué. A fine, even
weave background fabric was chosen
for the background and white organza for
the appliqué motifs. The turnings on
these fine fabric motifs were trimmed
narrowly and neatly to prevent them
showing through, and a variety of
decorative stitches were used to
embroider the flowers.

Stitch library

1

5

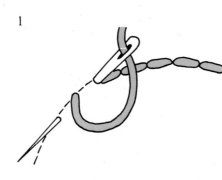

2

6

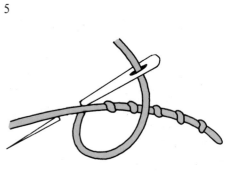

3

7

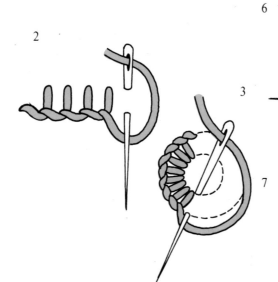

4

8

Fig. 1 Backstitch
Fig. 2 Blanket stitch
Fig. 3 Buttonhole stitch
Fig. 4 Chain stitch
Fig. 5 Couching
Fig. 6 Fishbone stitch
Fig. 7 Cross stitch
Fig. 8 Feather stitch

148

9
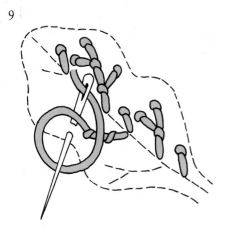

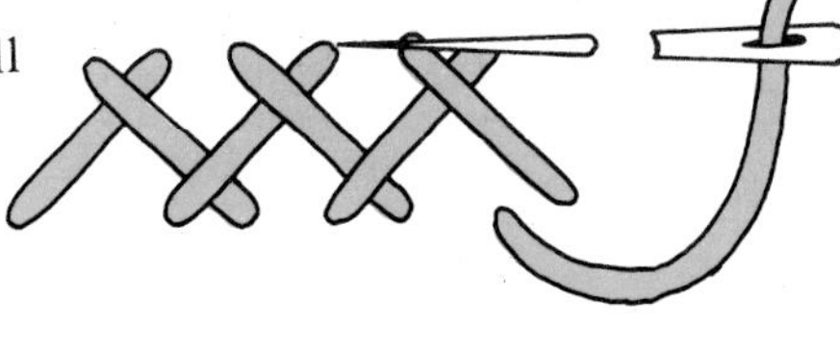

12

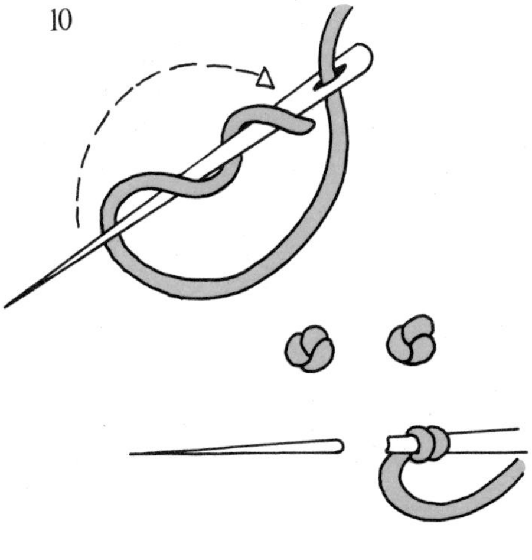

10
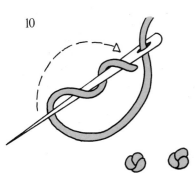

13
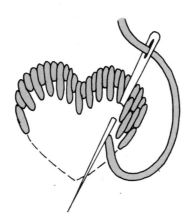

11

14
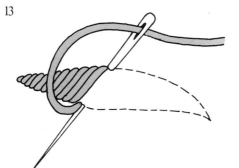

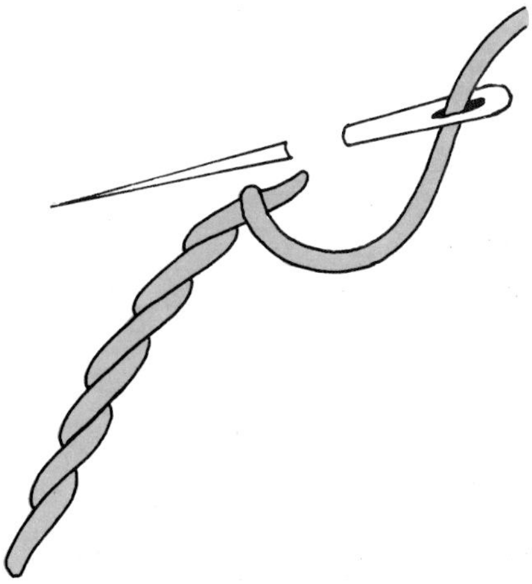

Fig. 9 *Coral stitch*
Fig. 10 *French knots*
Fig. 11 *Herringbone stitch*
Fig. 12 *Long and short stitch*
Fig. 13 *Satin stitch*
Fig. 14 *Stem stitch*

Glossary

Appliqué perse, (or Persian embroidery). A type of appliqué using motifs cut from printed fabric and sewn to a plain background fabric.

Bag, to To join two pieces of fabric by sewing them together, right sides facing, leaving a gap along one edge, and pulling the article right side out through the gap. The remaining raw edges are turned under and slip stitched.

Block method, or design A type of patchwork in which the whole article (e.g. a quilt) is made up of a number of patchwork patterns stitched together—as contrasted with an all-over design.

Collage A technique of forming pictures or designs by gluing fabric, paper, or other materials to a background.

Couching An embroidery technique in which one or more threads, or a cord, is laid onto fabric and held in place with small stitches using another thread.

Crazy patchwork A type of patchwork using irregular shapes and a variety of colours. It is often richly embroidered.

Cut and stagger A type of patchwork, usually done by machine, in which strips are joined along their sides then cut crossways. The resulting patched strips are sewn together in an irregular design.

Cut paper appliqué A type of appliqué using motifs cut from patterns made by folding and cutting bits of paper.

Foundation fabric The fabric to which patches are applied in the pressed method (q.v.) of patchwork construction.

Isosceles triangle A triangle in which two of the sides are equal—a shape used in some patchwork.

Masterpiece quilt Traditionally, a very fine patchwork quilt made by an accomplished needlewoman and generally reserved for the guest room.

Mayflower (Cathedral Window) patchwork A type of patchwork in which squares of printed fabric are sewn onto a plain foundation fabric (or vice versa) which has been cut and folded so as to create a three-dimensional effect.

Mitre To turn under the edges of a corner in such a way that the shape is preserved and the turnings are invisible.

Piecing The sewing together of patchwork shapes with a seam, to construct either a block or an all-over design.

Pressed method A type of patchwork construction in which the individual patches are sewn onto a background fabric, completely covering it.

Protractor A semi-circular flat instrument used for measuring angles.

Reverse appliqué A type of appliqué in which two or more layers of fabric are placed together and the design formed by cutting out shapes from the top layer downward, revealing the layers underneath.

Rhomboid A four-sided geometrical figure, sometimes used in patchwork, in which only opposite sides and angles are equal.

San Blas appliqué A colourful and intricate type of reverse appliqué (q.v.).

Sash work A type of block patchwork (q.v.) in which the blocks are separated by strips of fabric, usually of a solid colour.

Setting The process of sewing finished patchwork blocks together.

Shadow appliqué A type of appliqué in which the fabric shapes are sewn to the underside of a transparent background fabric to form a design.

Straight grain The direction along which the lengthways and crossways threads run in a fabric.

Suffolk Puffs [Yo Yo] An open type of patchwork consisting of gathered circles of fabric sewn together at their edges.

Template A shape cut from metal or cardboard used as a pattern in cutting fabric patches or shapes for appliqué.

Trapezium [trapezoid] A four-sided figure, sometimes used in patchwork, which has two parallel sides.

Wadding [batting] A soft carded material, often of cotton and available in various thicknesses. It is used to pad quilts, as well as other soft furnishings and garments.

Opposite: A detail from the child's cot quilt on page 75. In this four-patch block the appliquéd sections have been worked by hand, and the hexagons have been pieced together and applied to the background squares. The quilting has been hand worked, following the outlines of the individual shapes.

Index

Pictures supplied by
E. Alexander 130
Balmer/Courtesy of The American Museum,
Bath 1, 13, 82, 83, 112
Barkers of Lanecost 131
Theo Bergstrom 113
Steve Bicknell 9, 24, 66, 75BL, 116
Michael Boys/Susan Griggs Agency 32/3,
33BL, 33BR, 42/3
Camera Press 28, 34, 36/7, 41BL, 45, 46, 51,
59, 61TL, 61TR, 62, 67, 69, 72, 114
Victoria Carter 134
Martin Chaffer 29, 40
Alan Duns 61BR
Geoffrey Frosh 92
Melvin Grey 73, 75TL
Nelson Hargreaves 64/5
Steve Herr 19, 56T
Colin Jones 118
Peter Kibbles 71
Chris Lewis 2/3, 4/5, 47, 78, 106, 119, 122,
124/5, 128/9, 129
Sandra Lousada 52/3, 138, 139
Maison de Marie Claire/Dirand 38, 76/7
Susan Maxwell 84, 84/5, 94
Dick Miller 90, 117BL
G. Murrell 137
Julian Nieman 108/9, 110
Paf International 39 TL, 98
Chris Pierce 89
Roger Phillips 63
Spike Powell 21
Peter Pugh-Cook 20, 70, 77, 98/9, 100, 101,
102, 102/3, 126, 127
Iain Reid 132
Rex Features 87
Ruth Rutter 48
Kim Sayer 120, 121L, 121R
John Swannell 140
Syndication International 61
Transworld 10, 50/1, 74
Jerry Tubby 56B
Courtesy of the Victoria and Albert Museum/
Crown Copyright 54, 81

Liz Whiting 14
Liz Whiting/Lavinia Press 16/17
Michael Wickham 22

Artwork
Victoria Drew 35TR, 41, 45, 86, 95
Barbara Firth 47
Paul Kemp 6, 37, 39, 40
Trevor Lawrence 15, 71, 109
Chris Le Gee 38, 39,49
Coral Mula 111
Gwen Simpson 25, 26, 27, 28, 32, 34, 35, 38,
39, 40, 41, 44, 45, 48, 49, 50, 100
Joy Simpson 97
Paul Williams 63

Designers
E. Alexander 130
Linda Allison 11
Tricia Kerr Cross 115
Janna Drake 20
Joan Gilbert 105
Dorothea Hall 70
Pat Harman 134
Eleanor Harvey 120, 126
Suzy Ives 78
Lorraine Johnson 90
Anna Kinsey 106
Patty Knox 4
Sarah Lewis 127
Pauline Liu 132
Frances Newell 133
Patsy North 100
Faith Lloyd Phillips 71
Bridin Potts 131
Angela Salmon 137, 140
Caroline Sullivan 52
Pamela Tubby 139
Helen Tynan 150
Lindsay Vernon 103
Virginia Walters 98